COMBAT MISSIONS
FROM THE COCKPIT

▼A Jaguar four-ship showing the wide range of weapons options as external fits, from laser-guided bombs (LGB) to standard 1,000lb bombs, plus AIM-9L missiles and the Phimat chaff/flare pod. (BAe)

COMBAT MISSIONS
FROM THE COCKPIT

KEN DELVE

ARMS AND
ARMOUR

First published in Great Britain in 1990 by Arms & Armour Press Ltd, Villiers House, 41/47 Strand, London WC2N 5JE

Distributed in the USA by Sterling Publishing Co. Inc., 387 Park Avenue South, New York, NY 10016-8810.

Distributed in Australia by Capricorn Link (Australia) Pty Ltd, P.O. Box 665, Lane Cove, New South Wales 2066

British Library Cataloguing in Publication data:
Combat Missions: from the cockpit
  1. Great Britain. Royal Air Force
  I. Delve, Ken
    358.400941

ISBN 0-85368-963-6

Edited and designed by Roger Chesneau

Typeset by Typesetters (Birmingham) Ltd

Printed in Spain by Graficromo

GLOSSARY

AAA	Anti-aircraft artillery. In modern terms this usually refers to the rapid-fire, multi-barrel, radar-laid, mobile systems such as the Soviet ZSU-23/4.
AAM	Air-to-air missile. Refers to both radar and infra-red guided airborne missiles which are designed to engage other aircraft.
AAR	Air-to-air refuelling. The capability of taking on fuel from another aircraft whilst airborne.
AD	Air defence. Any element designed to operate against air threats but more commonly used to refer to the role of fighter aircraft.
AEW	Airborne early warning. A part of the overall AD system designed to 'fill in' the gaps left by ground-based radars and extend the overall radar coverage.
AFTS	Advanced Flying Training School. The second phase of pilot training.
ALARM	Air-Launched Anti-Radiation Missile. A weapon designed to counter the threat from ground-based, radar-laid AAA and SAM systems by attacking and destroying the radars themselves.
AS	Anti-ship/anti-shipping. The use of air-launched weapons against surface targets.
ASAP	As soon as possible. Used in a wide variety of contexts where an immediate response is required, e.g. on a CAS tasking message where the ground troops want airborne help *now*!
ASW	Anti-submarine warfare. Passive (detection and tracking) and active (attacking) operations against sub-surface targets.
ATM	Air Tasking Message. A NATO standard system of tasking aircraft for a particular mission.
BAI	Battlefield air interdiction. Air operations against targets which have a direct affect on the battlefield but which do not involve troops actually in contact, e.g. against a bridge over which reinforcements might arrive in the battle area.
BFTS	Basic Flying Training School. The initial part of pilot training.
BITE	Built-in test equipment. Most modern systems contain this internal monitoring circuitry as 'health checks' on serviceability.
BVR	Beyond visual range. Radar-guided AAMs have the capability to engage targets well outside the range at which a crew could visually identify or engage the target.
CAD	Concealed Approach and Departure. Used in the SH roles to refer to tactical operations where the location of the LZ must be kept secret.
CAP	Combat air patrol. A designated area which an AD aircraft uses as a reference point.
CAS	Close air support. Missions which are carried out in direct support of, and with influence upon, the immediate area of the battle.
CPT	Cockpit Procedural Trainer. A mock-up of an aircraft cockpit used for crew familiarization with cockpit layout, switches and drills.
DH	Delta-Hotel. Used in bombing to refer to a direct hit – the bomb actually striking the target.
DZ	Drop Zone. Designated point on the ground for the dropping of supplies or troops.
ECM	Electronic countermeasures. See below.
ESM	Electronic support measures. See below.
EW	Electronic warfare. The EW elements in the electronic side of the modern battlefield, as far as an aircraft is concerned, will comprise ESM and ECM, the former to detect and the latter to counteract air and ground threats. To complicate the matter comes ECCM – electronic counter-countermeasures! The idea here is to prevent the opposition's ECM effecting your systems . . . and so it goes on – a real game of trying to keep one step ahead.
FAC	Forward Air Controller. Usually refers to the ground controller who coordinates the CAS missions in a particular area.
FEAF	Far East Air Force. RAF Command in the Far East.
FEBA	Forward Edge of the Battle Area. In essence, the front line.
FJ	Fast jet. All single-seat and two-seat tactical and AD aircraft.
FLIR	Forward-looking infra-red.
FLOT	Forward Line of Own Troops.
FOD	Foreign object damage. Refers to any material which can possibly cause accidental damage to an aircraft.
FTS	Flying Training School.
GCI	Ground-controlled intercept(ion).
GLO	Ground Liaison Officer. Army officer attached to a tactical squadron.
HAS	Hardened aircraft shelter.

CONTENTS

HOTAS	Hands-on-throttle-and-stick. A system whereby essential controls are incorporated on the control column and throttle to make cockpit management simpler by enabling the pilot to make all the required 'switchery' without taking his hands off the two primary controls.		ORBAT	Order of Battle. Organization and numbers of a particular service (e.g., Polish Air ORBAT would refer to the Polish Air Force).
HUD	Head-up display. Primary flight, navigation and weapon data are projected on to the front screen of the canopy and focused at infinity so that it is superimposed on the outside world.		OS	Offensive support.
			OTR	Operational turn-round. Rapid re-arming and refuelling of combat aircraft.
INS	Inertial navigation system.		PBF	Pilot (or Personnel) Briefing Facility. Hardened shelter used as a squadron operations/planning/briefing centre.
IOC	Initial Operational Capability. The date at which an aircraft or system reaches operational status with its first unit.		PI	Photographic Interpreter.
IP	Initial Point. An easily identified ground point from which a target run commences (called TAP by the tactical Hercules squadrons, to whom IP is impact point).		PK	Probability of a kill. The assessment of the percentage chance of a missile or system achieving a lethal hit on its target.
			PODS	Pilot Op Data System.
IRD	Infra-red decoy. A flare ejected by aircraft to present a hot target to IR missiles and so protect the aircraft itself.		POL	Petrol, oil and lubricants. Target category covering the location of any one of these substances.
IRLS	Infra-red line scan. Camera system using specialized film which detects heat differentials.		RIC	Reconnaissance Intelligence Centre.
			RV	Rendezvous.
LZ	Landing zone.		SA	Strike/attack. Mission or aircraft designation covering both conventional and nuclear capability.
LRMTS	Laser ranger and marked-target seeker.			
MAD	Magnetic Anomaly Detector. System fitted to Nimrod aircraft to detect fluctuations in the magnetic field such as might be caused by the presence of a submarine.		SA	Semi-active. Refers to radar-guided missile which requires the radar to illuminate the target all the way to impact.
			SAM	Surface-to-air missile.
ME	Multi-engine. An aircraft with two or more engines.		SAR	Search and rescue.
MLU	Mid-life update. Most aircraft enter a period when major changes are required in order to maintain their front-line effectiveness. Complex programmes are usually grouped together as an MLU rather than as routine modifications.		SAP	Simulated Attack Profile. A 'dry' attack (i.e., one with no weapon release) on a training target, not on a designated weapon range.
			SEAD	Suppression of enemy air defences. Operations designed to counter the capability of the enemy ground-based air defence systems.
MMS	Missile Management System.		SLIR	Sideways-looking infra-red (system).
MP	Maritime patrol.		SRM	Short-range missile. A close-in AAM such as the Sidewinder.
MR	Maritime reconnaissance.			
MRM	Medium-range missile.		s.t.	Static thrust.
NATO	North Atlantic Treaty Organization.		TABS	Total Avionics Briefing System.
NOE	Nap-of-the-Earth, Ultra-low flying whereby the aircraft hugs the contours of the ground.		TAP	Target Acquisition Point.
			TAF	Terminal Airfield Forecast. Weather forecast for an airfield predicted for a given period.
NVG	Night vision goggles. Low-light device which enables a pilot to fly visually at low level during the night.			
OCA	Offensive counter-air. Operations designed to disrupt the enemy's air capability by attacking his airfields.		TFR	Terrain-following radar. System fitted to Tornado GR.1 which gives the aircraft an automatic terrain-avoidance capability.
OCU	Operational Conversion Unit. Training unit responsible for converting crews to aircraft type.		TOT	Time on target.
			VCR	Video cassette recorder.
OLF	Operational low flying. Low flying training at 100ft.		VDU	Video display unit.

PREFACE

This book does not pretend to be a definitive work on the Royal Air Force or even give the reader the full story of each of the aircraft types covered: rather, it is an attempt to 'put the reader in the cockpit' by examining a selection of the RAF's (and thus any modern military air arm's) current roles. Each of the roles is given a historical perspective to help set the scene, along with a few words on the aircraft type and likely future developments. However, the major part of each section describes a fictitious mission from inception to conclusion. Whilst the author has tried to keep 'jargon' to a minimum – all air crews talk in jargon, often with a stream of mnemonics which are meaningless to those outside of that particular sphere – some terms have been allowed to remain, since to exclude them would remove all sense of reality. For all aircraft which operate in the low-level tactical environment, there are many similarities in the way missions are planned and executed, but to avoid repetition much of the basic procedure has been bypassed, particular elements being highlighted for the different roles. The photographs have been chosen to illustrate the important aspects of each mission, and this has often meant 'switching' the squadrons around as the stories unfold (creating, in places, the odd pictorial hiatus). The missions follow the procedures and techniques used by the squadrons, but for reasons of security certain things obviously have to be left unsaid – although not, it is hoped, to the detriment of the accounts as a whole.

The mission narratives originated from discussions with air crews involved, and my thanks go to the many who have patiently sat through interviews and provided 'the personal touch'. None of the missions are specific to a particular squadron, and there are slight variations in the tactics and procedures used by different squadrons which I am sure the 'expert' eye will spot. My thanks especially, then, to the following units for their help: No 1(F) Squadron, No 7 Squadron, No 25 Squadron, No 27 Squadron, No 41 Squadron, No 42(TB) Squadron, No 47 Squadron and No 101 Squadron. The photographic material has come from a wide variety of sources and is appropriately credited, but I would particularly like to thank Rick Brewell, Paul Jackson, Gordon Bartley and Ian Black, and also British Aerospace, Marconi Underwater Systems and Hunting Engineering Ltd. To anyone I have missed out – my apologies, and I hope you will still talk to me!

Ken Delve
RAF Finningley

▶*A development of the Tornado GR.1, the F.2 Air Defence Variant (ADV) entered service in 1984 as the RAF's long-range interceptor for the 1990s. The definitive version now serving with all the front-line squadrons is the F.3, which has an improved capability and better performance. (BAe)*

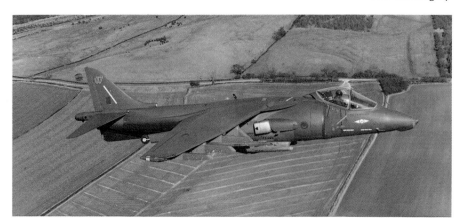

◀*Nozzles fully aft, the Harrier becomes a true combat aircraft of high subsonic performance. The bulbous canopy gives tremendous all-round visibility – including a view of the important rear sector.*

THE CHANGING FACE OF THE ROYAL AIR FORCE

I T IS VITAL for any military air arm to modernize and keep abreast of ever-changing technology, but the pace of technological advancement is now so rapid, and its cost so high, that it is often impossible for this to be achieved. Nevertheless, the 1980s saw a remarkable change in the face of the Royal Air Force, such that the ORBAT (Order of Battle) at the end of the decade was vastly different from that at its beginning. This programme was originally to have been completed by 1990, but a number of factors have delayed its full implementation by a few years. Gone are many of the long-serving (and well-loved) aircraft and in their place there is a new generation of high-tech aircraft – and a complete new dictionary of terms. However, although the machines have changed, the roles to be performed have not. The purpose of this book is to take the reader inside a modern military air force by looking at the various roles which that air force has to perform. These roles are considered in turn, the central theme of each being the execution of a typical mission.

FAREWELLS – AND CONTINUITY

The aircraft which vanished from RAF front-line service during the 1980s were the Canberra, Vulcan and Lightning, while others such as the Jaguar, Phantom and Buccaneer have lost their earlier importance as they have been replaced in their respective roles by the Tornado in its various guises. The re-equipment programme should have been even further down the line by 1990, with more Phantom squadrons converting and the venerable Shackleton being replaced by its airborne early warning (AEW) successor, the ill-starred Nimrod AEW (which has now given way to the E-3 Sentry, though at the cost of a delay in the schedule). At the present (planned) rate of re-equipment, the changeover will be complete by the latter part of 1992 – although this will herald but a short-term period of stability as towards the end of the decade EFA (European Fighter Aircraft, or Eurofighter) is due to enter service.

*

In May 1989 the Canberra celebrated the 40th anniversary of the type's first flight. Since it opened the era of jet bomber operations for the RAF on its introduction to service in 1951, the Canberra, in a wide variety of marks for an even wider range of roles, has served with no fewer than 63 RAF squadrons plus an almost endless number of special and trials units. Although designed as a traditional bomber aircraft, albeit one with a far greater speed and operational ceiling compared to its predecessors, the true value of the Canberra proved to be its ability to adapt to almost any role. During its front-line service the type served as a bomber (conventional and nuclear), an interdictor (with guns, rockets and air-to-surface missiles) and a photo-reconnaissance (PR) aircraft, with a capability from over 60,000ft to ultra-low level, day or night. Canberras were based, and operated, worldwide and during the 1950s and 1960s the aircraft was one of the RAF's most important weapon systems. Active service came in Malaya and Indonesia in the period 1955–65, and in the Suez War of

▼*From its original concept as a high-level bomber, the Canberra went on to become a true multi-role aircraft. One of its most successful applications was as a low-level interdictor, as exemplified by this B(I)8.*

▶ The last of the Canberra series, and the version that will serve on into the twenty-first century as a strategic recce aircraft – the PR.9.

▶ The unique delta-winged Avro Vulcan became part of the strategic deterrent with its stand-off nuclear weapons. The original white scheme gave way to grey and green when the aircraft switched to low-level penetration techniques.

1956, during which time only one aircraft was lost to enemy action. However, from the late 1950s the Canberra was gradually replaced by such aircraft as the Vulcan, Jaguar and Buccaneer – although many ex-Canberra crewmen would argue that none of these aircraft had the same overall capability as their predecessor.

Two front-line units survived into the 1980s, both operating PR variants. However, the disbandment of No 39 Squadron at RAF Wyton in May 1982 brought the front-line life of the Canberra to an end, although a number of that unit's PR.9s were organized as No 1 PRU (Photographic Reconnaissance Unit) to continue the strategic and survey roles. Neither squadron, however, was replaced in its full range of commitments, and as a result there was a distinct gap in the RAF's, and NATO's, recce capability. Two Canberra squadrons are still in service in support roles, one as an ECM training unit (No 360 Squadron) and the other as a target facility unit (No 100 Squadron). Both are destined to remain operational until the mid or late 1990s, while the PRU is likely to stay in existence until the early years of the new century and thus give the Canberra an unequalled 50 years of RAF service.

*

One of the star performers of the air show circuit is the last remaining RAF Vulcan, XH558. The decision to retain this aircraft is an unusual tribute since only rarely does the RAF maintain one of its former front-line types merely for display purposes! Designed to a 1947 specification, the Vulcan was one of the trio of 'V-bombers' with which Bomber Command sought to bring its heavy bomber fleet into the jet age and it entered service in July 1956. Its original role was that of a high-altitude strike (nuclear) bomber as part of the strategic defence system, but it also had a very useful 21,000lb conventional capability. Changing patterns of air defence meant that the Vulcans had later to adapt to low-level penetration techniques. A concise yet very accurate picture of life in a Vulcan at 200ft and 300kt is given by a former crew member:

◀ The last of a breed: XH558, the sole remaining flying Vulcan, tours the air shows as a tribute to the aircraft and in recognition of its popularity with the spectators.

▼ A thoroughbred fighter, the Lightning was years ahead of its contemporaries when it entered service as the RAF's first supersonic interceptor.

Once we get down to lower levels at moderately high air speeds the Vulcan feels solid and well illustrates the meaning of the word 'inertia'. The big rigid wing also gives little cushioning of the ride in the turbulent low-level air, particularly at high speed. The folks in the 'black hole' suffer most from this effect, as not only have they no visibility or horizon, but they have to sit facing rearwards in a hot and uncomfortable office.

A total of 134 B.1s and B.2s were built and served with nine RAF units in the UK and Cyprus, but there could be no doubt that by the late 1960s the Vulcan had become somewhat of a 'dinosaur of the air' in the face of ever-improving air defence systems. Even the change to low-level penetration techniques was of limited tactical value, although a Vulcan in a steep turn, diving down into a valley to vanish from sight, was an impressive manoeuvre! A follow-on strike/attack aircraft had been on the cards for many years, but the 1960s, thanks to political mismanagement, marked a low point in British defence procurement: the cancellation of the TSR.2 in 1965 left a great hole in the future capabilities of the RAF, the 'sanctuary' of an F-111 purchase proved to be only a fleeting fancy as that too passed under the axe, and the RAF was left with no option but to make the best of what was available. The net result was that no new aircraft could possibly enter service to replace the Vulcan for at least ten years, it being accepted that modern aircraft take about that time to progress from concept to IOC (Initial Operational Capability). So, despite the signing of agreements in the late 1960s for a new collaborative project, the Multi-Role Combat Aircraft (MRCA), the Vulcan would have to soldier on into the 1970s, and perhaps beyond.

The aircraft's only operational employment came at the very end of its life with conventional bombing raids on Port Stanley airfield during the Falklands conflict of 1982. Aircraft were also modified for the SEAD (suppression of enemy air defences) role with Shrike missiles to 'take-out' enemy raiders – a role in which they achieved a number of successes. By December 1982 the last of the bomber squadrons had disbanded as the run-up of the Tornado force commenced. However, that same year six aircraft were converted to K.2 standard to supplement the air-to-air refuelling force. It was these aircraft which were the last to go: No 50 Squadron disbanded in March 1984, thereby ending the era of big RAF bombers.

*

As the reheats kick in behind me the Lightning turns ever more tightly and I roll out about four miles behind my target, accelerating now, under the enormous power of the Rolls-Royce Avons . . . In missile range now, so I fire and immediately pull up and turn . . .

An aircraft which many would like to see on show again, and one which has a tremendous following, is the Lightning, described by some writers as the last of the true fighters. The demise of the last Lightning squadron in 1988 truly marked the end of an era: for the first time since the birth of the genre the RAF was left with no single-seat fighter. From the same design stable as the Canberra, the type started life as a supersonic research aircraft, eventually entering squadron service in 1960. As the RAF's first supersonic fighter, or rather interceptor, it outperformed all-comers but had a somewhat troubled existence. For most of its service life it was 'about to be phased out' in favour of a replacement but was continually reprieved, upgraded and kept in the front line. In due course a variety of marks served with seven RAF squadrons, and nearly 30 years after its IOC its performance of Mach 2.1 equalled that of many of the latest generation of fighters. However, its weapon system was so outdated that the aircraft's replacement finally became a matter of urgency: the Lightning had become a very expensive way of sending a pair of obsolete missiles not very far away! But, for all of those who ever fought against the Lightning, it could never be said that it was totally outclassed – there was many a murky day down low over the North Sea when an 'intruder' would be 'bounced' from below by a shark-like predator which would then accelerate away into the distance.

*

Although only twenty years old(!), the Jaguar has been withdrawn from its prime position as the RAF's main strike/attack aircraft and replaced by the Tornado. The RAF continues to operate three squadrons at Coltishall (Nos 6 and 54 in this role and No 41 in the tac-recce role), plus No 226 OCU at Lossiemouth. An Anglo-French project for an advanced trainer and close support aircraft, the design was upgraded to an all-weather attack aircraft early in its development. The Jaguar entered service in 1973 and within two years had replaced the Phantom as the main element of the RAF Germany strike wings. Its career here proved to be brief if intensive, however, since by mid-1985 the last of the Jaguar SA squadrons had gone, leaving just the tac-recce aircraft of No 2 Squadron in Germany. Despite a bad press which continually sniped at the aircraft for being underpowered, the Jaguar was very popular with its pilots. True, with a full external fit of bombs and tanks the aircraft was never going to perform as a

▼With the disbandment of the Binbrook Wing as its squadrons re-equipped with the Tornado F.3, Lightning – the last single-seat fighter in the RAF – bowed out. The overwing tanks seen here were an attempt to increase the range of the aircraft, especially during ferry trips. (Paul Jackson)

▼▶The RAF's next single-seat fighter? The European Fighter Aircraft (or Eurofighter) has been designed for the air superiority role to take the European partner air arms into the twenty-first century. It has also been proposed as a replacement in the OS roles for such aircraft as the Jaguar, but the validity of a very expensive, one-man aircraft in this environment must be seriously questioned. Due to enter service in the late 1990s, the EFA is already encountering political difficulties. (BAe)

fighter, but the fact is that it was never designed to do so. The aim of the bombing game is to hit a target on time not to get involved in air combat. To this end the Jaguar had much in its favour, not least of which was its small size. To pick up a Jag visually at low level, especially from head on, is very difficult and if you didn't pick it up early enough to turn in for an attack then it was often best to break away and find someone else to pester! One of the chapters in this book looks at the tactical recce role of the RAF's Jaguars.

*

The F-4 Phantom is without doubt one of the greatest aircraft of all time: 30 years old, over 5,000 built, and still in service with countless air arms around the world – and likely to remain so for another twenty years! A mid-1950s design, the F-4 entered service in 1961 although it was not until 1968 that the RAF jumped on to the F-4 bandwagon with deliveries to No 228 OCU. A total of 118 were issued to the RAF for use in the all-weather ground attack and recce roles. Gradually the Phantom took on more responsibility for the air defence role as new low-level types such as the Jaguar and Harrier were introduced – much to the chagrin of the F-4 'mud movers' who considered that their jet was a supreme exponent of the art of ground attack. With the phasing out of the Royal Navy's fleet carrier force and (temporarily, as it happened) fixed-wing aviation element, the Senior Service's FG.1s were handed over to the Royal Air Force.

From the late 1960s to the late 1970s some fourteen squadrons operated the type, increasing to fifteen with the arrival of the F-4Js of No 74 Squadron in 1984. Since the introduction of the Tornado F.3, the F-4 force has been gradually run down, and within the next two years only the squadrons at Wattisham, Mount Pleasant and Wildenrath will remain.

With its unusual flying characteristics the F-4 could be a 'bit of a pig' to fly in certain conditions, and it was not a very forgiving aircraft, but in practised

◄ The cockpit of the future. This view of the EAP (Experimental Aircraft Programme) development aircraft cockpit reflects the style and technology being incorporated into EFA, with multi-function screens and systems as the key elements. (BAe)

◄ For a short time the Jaguar was the central element of the strike/attack force in RAF Germany. (BAe)

hands it could be made to perform outstandingly well – often seen as a question of brute power over aerodynamics! The back-seater was offered only a limited view of the world because of the amount of 'ironwork' around the canopy, but the internal set-up was nevertheless quite good, despite the lack of a nav kit except in those aircraft with an inertial nav (IN). The Phantom is remembered with affection by those who flew it, and it has been assessed as the ultimate multi-role aircraft of its time – a fair summing up of an aircraft that is by no means finished!

Although the Phantom will remain active in the air defence (AD) role until the latter part of the 1990s (much to the delight of those who fly it and consider it an unsurpassed exponent of combat flying), as an overall weapons system it represents increasingly elderly technology. The ever more sophisticated electronic environment and the introduction of third (virtually fourth) generation fighters by the Warsaw Pact (WarPac) make the F-4's task much harder and its projected kill ratio that much lower. The overall AD scenario will change with the introduction of the Eurofighter in the late 1990s as this aircraft will both complement the BVR (beyond-visual-range) capability of the Tornado F.3 and prove to be an agile combat aircraft in the overland close defence role – although its employment as an OS (offensive support) aircraft to replace the Jaguar is perhaps more questionable. The project is well advanced, although, like all collaborative schemes, it is prone to political machinations, especially in view of the changing political scene in Eastern Europe and the pressure for a reappraisal of long-term armament programmes.

*

▼ One of the most successful aircraft of all time, the F-4 Phantom has been in service for more than 30 years, and although now getting old in terms of its technology it is still a very potent weapon system.

Another of the great 'workhorses' which has been partially replaced is the Buccaneer. A naval aircraft that the RAF took up almost as an afterthought, the Buccaneer did not enter RAF service until 1970 – twelve years after its first flight and seven years after the Navy had commenced carrier operations with the

type. Nevertheless, it proved to be a versatile and robust aircraft suited both to the overland strike role it performed in Germany and the maritime strike/attack (anti-shipping) role. In the overland low-level penetration role, settled down at 600kt and at 100ft, the aircraft seemed to be in its element, giving a smooth ride and yet, despite its size, being remarkably responsive to the controls – 'like sitting back in an armchair'. Thanks to the offset and slightly raised position of the rear seat the nav even had good all-round visibility. Many a missile operator on 'Red Flag' exercises has recorded his amazement at the gyrations performed by the 'Bucc' at 50ft over the desert and the impossibility of his getting a shot away – the old idea of fast and low!

Equipping two operational squadrons at Lossiemouth (Nos 12 and 208), the Buccaneer remains the sole dedicated maritime strike/attack aircraft on the RAF inventory. The anti-ship role also seems to suit this solid aircraft (it was, after all, designed for carrier ops) as it can get even lower over the waves as it bores in towards its target at a great rate of knots. There is nowhere to hide over

▲ *The Buccaneer has also been employed in the 'buddy-buddy' (tactical) tanker role, equipped with a hose unit in the bomb bay. (Paul Jackson)*

▼ *Low-level over the sea – home to the maritime attack Buccaneers in their anti-shipping role. Now equipped with the Sea Eagle stand-off missile, the aircraft pack a powerful punch. (Paul Jackson)*

the sea, and as ship radars have improved so has the detection range and height. The basic trick now is to confuse and swamp – and fire your missiles from as far away as possible! The modern generation of AS missiles proved their effectiveness during 1982 with Exocet attacks against British warships off the Falklands. The Buccaneer's equivalent weapon is Sea Eagle, again a proven system, and a 'six-ship' of Buccs each with four missiles is a formidable prospect.

Many Bucc men are of the opinion that the best replacement for their aircraft, in any of its roles, is another Buccaneer with upgraded systems and weapons, but over the years the aircraft has had a number of fatigue problems

◄ A classic maritime patrol aircraft, the Shackleton was the culmination of Avro's series of large, four-engined aircraft which had started with the famous Lancaster.

and now has only a limited life-span left. No definite plans have been laid for a replacement, but Rumour Control suggests that the Tornado (after all, what else is there?) in one form or another will take over the anti-shipping role. This would be a very logical move as the German *Marineflieger* has been using a GR.1 variant in this capacity since 1982 and loudly sings its praises. British Aerospace has put forward a maritime version of the F.3, and this must be one of the prime candidates.

*

Another aircraft which celebrated its 40th birthday in 1989 was the venerable Shackleton. Developed from the Lincoln bomber, the prototype maritime reconnaissance (MR) Shackleton first flew in March 1949 and entered service in 1951. Fourteen squadrons operated the type between 1951 and 1972 with maritime patrol (MP) and anti-submarine warfare (ASW) as the primary roles; the last MR variant, the MR.3, had an operational range of over 3,500 miles and carried a variety of bombs, depth charges, torpedoes and sonobouys in its cavernous bomb bay. On at least one occasion the 'Shack' was called on to undertake a more conventional bombing role when No 42 Squadron dropped fragmentation bombs (and propaganda leaflets) on rebel tribesmen in Oman in 1957. In the gradual run-down of British forces worldwide, the Shackleton squadrons were among the first casualties.

However, the increased threat to the United Kingdom from low-level penetrating bombers revealed gaps in the country's radar coverage and it was decided to acquire an airborne early warning (AEW) radar system by refitting a number of Shackleton MR.2s. IOC for the 'new' AEW.2 was January 1972, the sole operator being No 8 Squadron. Apart from its radome, the distinctive feature of the variant is the 'spark plug' which sticks up from the fuselage!

◄ A number of 'Shacks' were modified as AEW aircraft to fill a gap in the UK radar chain coverage. These aircraft continue to soldier on pending the IOC of the proposed Boeing Sentry. (Paul Jackson)

The cancellation in 1986 of the Nimrod AEW.3 meant that the Shack had to be granted yet another extension to its operational life, the remaining aircraft continuing to provide vital AEW cover until the introduction in 1991 or 1992 of the Boeing E-3 Sentry.

THE FEATURED ROLES

The old saying 'Practice makes perfect' could be seen as the rationale behind all the training that squadrons undertake: if you can fly at 600kt and at 100ft around the Tactical Training Areas and find and hit your target, then there is an even chance that you will be able to do it 'for real'. If you have never tried it, then the chances are that you will either hit the ground or fly too high and get taken out by a SAM (surface-to-air missile). If you are bounced by a fighter, decisions have to be taken instantaneously: watch the fight, manoeuvre out of missile/gun parameters whilst trying to bring your own weapons to bear, and get the first shot away. It needs a knowledge of the capabilities of aircraft and systems and confidence in how to handle them. There is no second chance. The same logic applies to all areas of operational flying: if you don't train the right way in peacetime then it is *impossible* to achieve success during conflict. To quote the 'Top Gun' motto, 'You fight like you train'.

All these aspects will be examined in the following chapters although not all are covered in every mission; for example, a met brief is a met brief – most sorties start with one – and there would be little point in going over this same ground in each chapter. After met comes the planning stage (assuming that the met man got it right for your operational area), the nature of which varies according to mission and aircraft type. However, all low-level sorties start with target and route maps, usually drawn up in the old-fashioned way with a ruler and pen although most aircraft also have their own 'strike rule', a plastic gizmo of holes, curves and graduations aimed at simplifying the planning and saving time. For some that is the end of the planning, for others it is now time to get into the computer 'hot seat' and programme the route with 'green writing'. Armed with computer tape and map (just in case the aircraft computer dumps!), crews pitch in to the briefing. Again, this takes a variety of forms but the basic idea is the same – that everyone in the aircraft and/or formation is fully aware of the aim of the mission and how the latter is to be accomplished. A good sortie starts from sound planning and a thorough brief; miss either one of those, and problems lie ahead.

A final check with ops, kitting out in whatever flight gear is appropriate, and out to the aircraft. Here the crew find their warbird 'hot to trot'. This book

▼ *Operational training takes a wide variety of forms, and, as an integrated part of the alliance, the RAF trains as often as it can with its NATO partners. DACT (Dissimilar Air Combat Training) with a pair of Danish F-16s certainly sharpens the reflexes. (RDAF)*

cannot cover the incredible amount of hard work that goes on behind the scenes. Air crews only fly the aircraft, which really belong to the skilled technicians who make them work and 'loan' them out for short periods to these strange green-suited individuals. Thirty minutes later, or eight hours later, the aircraft are handed back, often with some part not working. By this time the aircraft is probably required for another mission and so the routine of the operational turn-round (OTR) gets underway – whatever snags have been reported are fixed and the fuel and weapons are replenished. Meanwhile, for the crew, the all-important debrief calls. Every minute of every sortie is valuable and contains its own lessons, lessons that are maximized by lengthy post-sortie debriefs which take the mission apart piece by piece – what went right, what went wrong, what could have been done better.

This should be the aim of every sortie from the routine daily mission at squadron level to the co-ordinated sortie package of one of the major tactical exercises such as 'Red Flag'. Most NATO nations take part in this series of exercises held in the Nellis Training Area in America's Nevada Desert. It is the nearest you can get to war without being shot at – and that is exactly how it was designed to be, the arbiter of training and tactics. Does the squadron tactic work? How do you face up to the fighter and SAM threat? To find out, try it. 'Red Flag' puts it all together. There is no room in this book to look at the wide range of NATO exercises or even to consider the increasing variety of 'Flag' exercises such as 'Copper' and 'Green', but the bottom line is that what happens in the missions outlined in the following chapters is the key: get the 'basics' right and then apply them to the operational scenario. You fight like you train.

GENERAL CONSIDERATIONS

To help the reader's understanding of certain aspects of the role analyses, a few general considerations will be covered here so that they will not have to be explained in the individual chapters.

The met brief

'A look at the synoptic chart shows a weak front passing over the southern half of the country, with high pressure over France and a ridge of high pressure extending over much of the country . . .' So much for the preamble to the met brief! Certainly, a glance at the chart shows that the weather should be quite reasonable for low-level around the UK. This is confirmed by the other met documents which show that there is little or no cloud over the country, except in the extreme north.

However, the most important part of the documentation is the TAFs – forecasts for individual airfields of what the weather will do over a given period of time. With a route that plans to enter low-level near Newcastle, a look at the TAF for Newcastle should prove instructive:

EGNT 0716 24014KT 9999 3CUO25

This translates as 'Newcastle between 0700 and 1600hr is expecting a wind of 240 degrees at 14kt, visibility greater than 10km and only three-eighths of cumulus cloud at 2,500ft – in other words, a very nice day to go low flying! Other airfields around the planned route are examined in similar fashion and all are giving a similar story, although one or two are suggesting deteriorations in the morning period down to 8,000m visibility and five-eighths cloud at 1,500ft. Matters can often be far more complicated, and in order to confirm that

◀One of the ultimate tests is to take part in the 'Flag' exercises over the Nellis Ranges in the United States. Every aspect of a unit's operational capability is tested in a very realistic scenario. (Flt Lt Nickles)

the forecasts are going as predicted the Actual Weather (issued hourly) for a particular airfield can be checked.

This wealth of met information allows the final decision to be made about where to go flying. If you have to go to a particular area for operational reasons, even though the weather does not look good, at least you are forewarned and can sketch out appropriate plans. (This sounds good in theory, but in practice it is often very different as the British weather frequently defies the best efforts of the met men and proves to be the complete opposite of that forecast!

Briefing

Every squadron has its own sets of standard briefing slides, and these are used to ensure that all the essential items are covered by the briefing crew; they also act as a reminder to the briefer of the items he should be covering! Not all the members of a formation can take part in every aspect of the planning and so the brief is the only way of getting everyone on the same wavelength and imparting the essential details of the mission. Up goes the 'Domestics' slide: 'You write whilst I talk' is the clue to copy down the pertinent details from the overhead projector (OHP) slide. Crew, aircraft, HAS (hardened aircraft shelter), call-signs, weapons and fuel details, times – all are written down on knee-pads for ready reference in the aircraft. If you are not happy with a particular aspect (Why does my aircraft have less fuel than everyone else's?), now is the time to query it.

Next comes the Route Brief, covering the route to and from the target area, heights, speeds, radar fixes and other navigation details and the general intelligence scenario. Hand out the 1:50,000 Initial Point (IP)-to-target maps and run through each one with details of aiming points, nav system references and reversionary sight settings just in case the automatics of the computer weapons-aiming do not work out. Then through the 'what ifs', with a look at the emergency procedures for selected scenarios. Different briefings require different specialist briefing details and thus many of the 'slides' will relate only to a particular aircraft or mission, for example the tactical plan for dealing with 'sorting' targets for an air defence aircraft or the load details for a Hercules drop. There are as many possibilities as there are aircraft and roles.

Radar principles

Many of the roles mention the use of radar to update the nav system or locate a target, and so a few words on general radar principles would seem to be appropriate. If you throw a ball at a wall it bounces back; if the wall were not there the ball would just keep on going and you would not get your ball back.

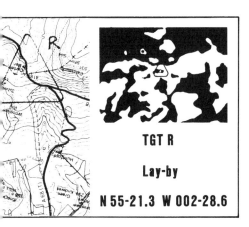

TGT R

Lay-by

N 55-21.3 W 002-28.6

radar can see and those which it cannot, and so they can be related to the ground as shown on the map.

In essence the radar beam is the ball being thrown out of the aircraft: if something gets in the way, be it the ground or another aircraft, then the beam is bounced back at the aircraft. This, of course, is a very simple analogy as there are many complex variations; however, the principle holds true. So, for the fighter looking for another aircraft in the great expanse of sky, it is simply a question of the radar transmitting a pulse (beam) and the aircraft looking for a returning pulse to arrive at the receiver. Having hit another aircraft, the pulse bounces off and returns, or at least some fraction of it does, back the way it came to be picked up by the aircraft receiver.

Thus the fighter can tell the direction of the target. By working out how long it has taken the pulse to travel out and back, the fighter can also calculate the range of the target. Both these items of information can then be displayed on a screen as a target position. Modern fighter aircraft, such as the Tornado F.3, no longer give a raw radar picture but use computers to provide a synthetic video image along with additional computed data, which helps to reduce the crew's workload and simplify the intercept.

The all-weather OS (offensive support) aircraft, such as the Tornado GR.1, use radar to update their navigation systems and for the terminal attack phase. The principle is the same as that outlined above except that the radar beam bouncing off the ground provides a much more complex picture and one which the navigator has to interpret to determine the area of interest. Using the nav kit to determine the approximate area of the fixpoint on radar, the navigator examines the display and relates the radar returns to the map of the fix area. In the Tornado the computer puts a cross on the radar display where it thinks the fixpoint is, the cross is moved to the interpreted position and this information is then inserted into the computer.

In the attack phase the radar is switched on again to refine the nav attack system and achieve the most accurate weapon delivery. Using offsets (i.e., predetermined points which are likely to show well on the radar and which have been referenced to the target position) and the target itself, the computer can be updated in the same way as it was for a fixpoint. Although modern nav/attack systems are very accurate, they still only provide estimated positional data, the reliability of which depends on how good the particular system is. Radar, by the very fact that it is looking at the real world outside the aircraft, provides data showing where the aircraft actually is rather than where the computer thinks it is. By updating the computer from the radar the crew get the best of both worlds.

▶ *All good sorties start from a good briefing (and vice versa). This is the time to get everyone on the same wavelength.*

FLYING TRAINING

WITH THE ESTABLISHMENT of an Air Battalion of the Royal Engineers in 1911 came the requirement to train pilots for its fixed-wing aeroplanes (No 2 Aeroplane Company). The following year brought the formation of the Royal Flying Corps and the realization that a training organization would have to be created. The first element, and perhaps the most important, was the creation of the Central Flying School (CFS) to provide basic training for pilots. However, for a variety of reasons it was decided that those wishing to take commissions in the RFC should first of all, and at their own expense, learn the rudiments of flying at one of the numerous civilian schools! Once 'qualified' they could apply for CFS and undergo the military course. This pattern of incorporating civilian schools into the training of military pilots has proved useful on a number of occasions, especially during expansion periods when the military training schools either did not exist or could not cope with the numbers of pupils.

The pilot wishing to join the 'front line' in 1913 was faced with a wide variety of types on which to learn but the basic concept was the same – to acquire piloting skills so that he could successfully operate an aircraft under a given number of conditions: get off the ground, fly around and land safely! It was often possible for a pilot to 'go solo' after less than an hour of instruction and to gain his 'wings' within a matter of hours.

As the war progressed so the call for pilots became even greater and the training 'empire' expanded to meet the need. A new factor was the growth of specialization as aircraft were developed or adapted to meet specific roles, including, towards the end of the war, that of long-range heavy bomber. The basic training for pilots varied little throughout the period as on-squadron training brought the pilot up to speed on a particular type for a particular role. For the other members of the crew there was virtually no training of any description.

The interwar period saw great changes in the training establishment although after the initial postwar run-down these were often cosmetic, involving merely an alteration to a unit's title. By 1920 the Flying Training School (FTS) system had stabilized, with five FTS units in the UK and, from 1921, one in Egypt. At the same time the specialist establishments such as the School of Aerial Gunnery and Bombing were integrated more firmly in the training organization.

It would be impossible, and unnecessary, in this book to try to describe the changes which took place in the RAF training organization during the period 1930–1950 save to say that the job of any training organization is to provide the output required by a user to the required standard and in the right numbers. It is a tribute to those who managed the training organization during the late 1930s and up to 1945 that they were, in general terms, able to achieve this primary aim. The 1940s in particular saw the growth of more complex aircraft which could no longer be operated by a single crewman but needed the combined efforts of a team of specialists (for example, two in the Mosquito night fighter, seven in the Lancaster) in order to achieve success. This in turn led to

▲ Perhaps the greatest pilot trainer of all time, the Harvard was used worldwide to train many thousands of personnel and served the RAF as the standard equipment of the FTSs for sixteen years from 1938. Designed as a robust machine capable of enduring the attentions of its students, the Harvard was outstanding in all respects and had very few vices.

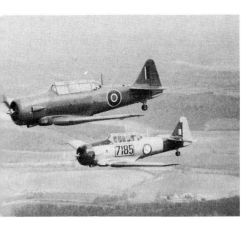

▶ Clear skies and a piece of free airspace – the joys of flying!

the growth of additional specialist training schools. Since 1945 the aircraft have changed but in the main the aircrew specializations have survived and developed.

THE PILOT

'Great pilots are made not born . . . A man may possess good eyesight, sensitive hands, and perfect coordination, but the end product is only fashioned by steady coaching, much practice, and experience.' This statement, by Air Vice Marshal 'Johnnie' Johnson, one of the greatest fighter pilots of the Second World War, encapsulates the RAF view of flying training and underwrites a proven system.

To reach an operational squadron a student pilot has to face a long and complex series of training courses – having first of all passed the hurdle of selection. From Day One to Combat Ready takes almost three years as the principles outlined above take their course and the basic skills are acquired, and a period consolidating those skills and progressing to new ideas and techniques follows. 'Streaming' takes place, students being selected for specific types of training and then following type- and role-related training, on the way to the final goal of arriving on a front-line squadron. But it all starts from the same point . . .

The aim of the Basic Flying Training School (BFTS) syllabus is 'to provide flying instruction, synthetic instruction and academic instruction to enable students to qualify for advanced flying training' – in other words, to take a student and try to establish whether he or she has the ability to become a military pilot, to assess in which area of military flying such ability lies and to provide the grounding for appropriate advanced training. The important consideration is that this is just the first step on the road to becoming a productive member of an operational squadron.

▼ The Shorts Tucano is replacing the Jet Provost as the RAF's basic trainer and introduces tandem-seating in place of the side-by-side arrangement of the JP.

Learn, assimilate, consolidate and move on – the routine of the training course. On the assumption that the student on Day One knows little or nothing about flying aeroplanes, there is no point in sticking him in the front seat of a Tucano and turning him upside down! There is nothing in civilian life which can provide much of a background to the skills which will now need to be developed: merely having to think in a three-dimensional environment provides plenty of food for thought. The classroom beckons, therefore, for the first few weeks, to enable the student to get to grips with the rudiments of aviation-related subjects: after a few hours of the Meteorology package the evening TV weather forecast takes on a different complexion as the rapidly approaching warm front quickly translates into warm-sector conditions of low cloud and poor visibility, which may well mean no flying. Then comes the instructor who endeavours to convince you that a huge piece of metal really does fly through the air: aerofoils, flight forces, lift and drag – a mass of scientific facts and figures and still no sign of a real aircraft to play with. And so the ground school continues, until at least enough has been passed on by the instructors to allow you to move to the next

23

stage – no, not an aircraft, but the next best thing: a simulator! Great use is made of synthetic trainers to reinforce the lessons of the classroom – for example computer programmes which consolidate the teaching of aircraft technical systems (the fuel system makes much more sense when animated on a computer screen) and a Cockpit Procedural Trainer (CPT) where basic drills can be practised and checks learnt in slow time. All these elements have but one function – to ensure that the time spent in the air is not wasted. Familiarity with basic procedures and techniques means that more time can be spent on the actual business of moving the aircraft through the sky.

The Tucano was introduced to the RAF's BFTS world in 1989 as the service's new basic trainer, replacing the Jet Provost. Although it is a turboprop aircraft, it is designed on the single-lever system to simulate jet operation. All previous basic trainers had been side-by-side as this was considered the best arrangement for both instruction and assessment: you could see what the student was doing wrong. The tandem arrangement of the Tucano is, therefore, a major change, and with the student in the front seat there is little the instructor can do to monitor closely how he attempts to achieve a particular manoeuvre. It is, however, a more appropriate environment for the potential fast-jet pilot and so is a better option for the future. The array of instruments and switches are almost second nature because of the extensive use of ground-based training aids, the ultimate of which is the flight simulator, and by the time the student takes off on his first flight the cockpit is familiar territory. It is often said that 50 per cent of brain capacity is left on the ground, and this makes it even more important to make the best use of that which remains!

The standard instructional technique is to reinforce the ground lessons by demonstrating that the theory does actually work and then letting the student practise until he is happy with it. Gradually the basics build up – how to fly the aircraft straight and level, turning without losing height and so on. Without these basic skills there can be no progress. The Tucano is a very responsive aircraft but is also reasonably stable and such basic exercises are soon mastered. Getting the aircraft airborne is easy – speed up and roll down the runway until the aircraft feels like taking to the air; landing, however, is not quite the same, and 'pounding the circuit' becomes the routine for most sorties.

Turn downwind . . . 'Charlie-two-four downwind to roll' . . . 'Charlie-two-four one ahead'. Check speed below 145kt, airbrake in and select landing gear down; gentle rumble as the gear extends and locks and the undercarriage indicators confirm that all three are locked down. Fuel contents okay, two pumps on and threshold speed calculated at 85kt, lock the seat harness and confirm that the parking brake is off, and that completes the landing checks.

Approaching the end of the downwind leg with the speed washing back towards 115kt . . . Turn as the runway vanishes under the trailing edge of the wing . . . Round the corner call 'Finals, three greens' . . . Play the turn to roll out lined up with the centreline of the runway with flap 'Down' and speed reducing towards threshold speed. Final check of toes clear of the brakes. With its responsive controls, Tucano is amongst the easiest of aircraft to fly, and land, making it an ideal training machine. Throttle back to 'Flight Idle' and check the rate of descent as the aircraft crosses the threshold and settles down on to the runway. Hold the nosewheel off by a bit of back pressure on the stick, throttle forward to about 60 per cent torque and the aircraft quickly takes to the air again . . . A bit of right rudder to counteract the yaw and, when safely away, up with the gear and flaps ready for the next circuit. The principles are the same for all aircraft; all that changes is the actual numbers. If you can't get it right now you never will!

After some 31 hours' flying comes the next major hurdle, the Progress Test. One sortie to confirm to the instructor that you have mastered the basics and are capable of proceeding to the next stage . . . Tick on the board and back into ground school for the applied phase: more facts and figures to learn, other manoeuvres to get to grips with and an introduction to such arts as navigation, formation flying and night flying. As this part of the course progresses the first set of decisions is made and after a few weeks the helicopter stream (or 'rotary-wing' as the official designation has it) is designated and begins its own lead-in course prior to departure to the helicopter training school. With the intermediate phase of just over 77 hours complete, the final streaming takes place between the fast-jet (FJ) and multi-engine (ME) elements. Both continue on the Tucano with their respective lead-in courses, which include low-level navigation, formation flying and a consolidation of all previous aspects.

The award of pilot's wings is the signal that part one of the road to squadron status is behind. It is a dividing of the ways for the different pilots: the rotary wing students have already left; the ME boys vanish to Finningley to join the Multi-Engine Training Squadron (METS); and the FJ candidates cross to the other side of the country to Valley for the Advanced Flying Training School (AFTS) and the superb Hawk trainer. To cover every aspect of every training course would take up more words than the length of this book permits and so, perhaps unfairly, our examination here will follow the FJ candidate.

With its operational performance the Hawk is in a different league from that of the Tucano, but the basic principles remain the same, as does the training routine. Hello and welcome to AFTS . . . Now sit down in this classroom and learn all about your new aircraft type. Engine (a jet this time), fuel, electrics, hydraulics, and so on . . . More facts and figures to learn, digest and remember. The basic training pattern is the same, with classroom lessons, synthetic training and extensive use of the simulator – the best place to learn how to deal with a complex aircraft emergency is safely on the ground in the 'sim' rather than in the middle of Wales on a dark wet night!

. . . Yet another tick on the board and a certificate in the flying log book, and then on to another course. With *x* hours already logged there is no doubt that you can fly an aeroplane, but can you fight it? The purpose of the next course is to make this transition. The Tactical Weapons Units at Chivenor and Brawdy both operate the Hawk and both have the same primary role of introducing FJ air crews to tactical weapons operating techniques, building on previous training and equipping the student for Operational Conversion Unit (OCU) training.

The aircraft may be the same but the way it is used is certainly very different and at last there is more of a 'squadron feel' to the course. The aircraft even look different: gone is the red and white paint scheme, replaced by a

▼ *With its superb performance, the Hawk takes the FJ student into the realms of high-speed/ high-g operations. As can be seen here, the visibility from the cockpit is excellent – a great advantage when it comes to formation flying!* (BAe)

green/grey OS or low-visibility grey style. Furthermore, these aircraft carry things – a 30mm gun pod on the fuselage centreline or practice bomb carriers (Carrier, Bomb, Light Store or CBLS) on the underwing pylons, the latter also being used for AIM-9L Sidewinder air-to-air missiles (AAM). However, for the first few days the aircraft are just glimpsed through the windows of the ground school classrooms! A short burst of lessons, a couple of simulator exercises and then out to the flight line and into the now familiar front seat of the Hawk. The remainder of the course is based around the squadron, and all subsequent ground schooling is run as phase briefs leading into each new part of the course. Not too many differences in the cockpit, except for the weapon 'switchery' and sighting system and so the 'left–right' cockpit checks from Valley days still work.

Over the ensuing weeks the course covers the basic techniques needed for low-level operations and weaponry (mainly strafing with the 30mm Aden cannon) along with an introduction to air combat. Not only does this provide a sound basis for further development in the advanced phase, it also enables another 'streaming' to be made. About half-way through the course the students are designated for either the OS or the AD role and each then follows a role-related advanced phase. For the OS pilots, guns lead to bombs with 3kg practice ordnance being thrown from either a shallow (10-degree) dive or level flight: line it up, pickle off the bomb . . . and then wait for the score from the range officer using the standard clock code and distance in feet away from the centre

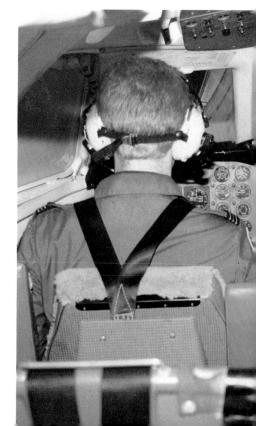

◄ To get above the cloud and have 30 minutes in which to 'indulge' in a bout of aerobatics is sheer delight. It also had the benefit of making you aware of the performance of your aircraft and develops the essential handling ability which comes with confidence. (BAe)

▲ For the student who has gone down the multi-engine route from BFTS, the Jetstream introduces all those essential aspects of handling and technique required by the RAF's 'heavy' aircraft such as Hercules and Nimrod. (T. Malcolm English)

▼ A great deal of time, however, is spent flying a box which is firmly rooted to the ground. Simulators are the best place to learn basic procedures (and to make basic mistakes).

of the target. Live weaponry is only part of the course, and a great deal of time is spent refining low-level nav techniques as a singleton and then as the more important low-level tactical pair. Learn to think about another aircraft: as Lead, you have to look after your No 2 and think what impact any changes of plan will have on him. Making full use of ground cover, each aircraft dips into small valleys and is lost from sight . . . Scan the sky, watch the ground, check the mission's progress, look across to pick up the No 2 and 'clear his tail' . . . Coming up to a turn, so get ready for a mutual protection manoeuvre designed to keep the area behind the aircraft under visual cover at all times.

The final low-level trips involve a pair with targets to hit (Simulated Attack Profiles, or SAPs), with a third Hawk lurking around as a 'bounce', playing the part of the enemy fighter. Now the eyes really are on stalks: any valley might be hiding the 'bounce', who will take great delight in sneaking up and shooting you in the back before running away again. The difference between living and being shot down depends on 'lookout', spotting the 'bounce' and reacting to negate his missile or gun attack.

After a hard, enjoyable and very necessary course comes a posting to yet another one, although at least this time the move is to an operational type. There are two types of FJ pilot, the single-seater of the Harrier and Jaguar and the front-seater of the Tornado, F-4 and Buccaneer. Again, we do not have space to follow the route of each individual but the basic principles are the same, with posting to an Operational Conversion Unit for the respective aircraft type. Yes, yet another course!

For Tornado GR.1 (i.e. strike/attack or, in the popular terminology, 'mud-movers') air crew, this means a move to a unique RAF base, the Tri-National Tornado Training Establishment (TTTE) at Cottesmore. Now the real work begins, and a reflection of the complex nature of the aircraft is the length and complexity of the ground school. Great use is made of part-task trainers and simulators to help crews get to grips with the aircraft systems and the almost unbelievable jungle of Tornado-related terminology – a web of CSAS, PFCS, SAHR, AFDS, TV/TAB, NAVWAMS, WCP and a host of other acronyms which would fill a book! TTTE is designed to convert the crew to the aircraft and there is plenty to occupy both front- and back-seaters as they try to sort out the bewildering array of buttons and lights which stare out from the grey panelling. Then comes the shock: it all works, so turn it off and see how you get on without it! Gone is the computer which does all the hard work and all the automatic targeting: it's back to map and stopwatch and an 'iron sight', just like it is on a Jet Provost or Hawk. Why bother? Simply, the answer is that you cannot turn back just because the nav kit waves goodbye – you still have to get to the target

27

on time and complete the mission. It's all part of the flexibility. Train a 'button-pusher' and that is what you will get – someone who can only push buttons.

For the boy in the front there is the very novel problem of having wings which move forwards and backwards. The Tornado handles superbly but, to the chagrin of many a pilot, on quite a number of sorties the navigator flies the aircraft from the back seat via the computer and autopilot or, alternatively, the terrain-following radar (TFR) is engaged and in combination with the autopilot flies the aircraft. Nevertheless, there is plenty of 'hands-on' time and the Tornado proves to be an excellent low-level aircraft as it pulls around the valleys at 450kt.

The next course is even tougher. Having learnt how to operate the aircraft you must now learn how to fight it in its operational role. This is the task of the Tornado Weapons Conversion Unit (TWCU) at Honington. The course is designed to introduce the crew to the weapons capability of the GR.1 and to develop tactical awareness. At this stage you become aware of the almost magical accuracy of the Tornado weapons system, and dropping 'DHs' (Delta-Hotels, i.e. direct hits) on the weapons ranges becomes second nature. When the kit malfunctions or when the bombs are not quite so good the usual answer is a 'switch-pigs' by one of the crew. Convinced that this aircraft is the best thing ever, the pilot now can join the squadron.

Made it at last? No, not quite yet, as there is still the matter of a six-month work-up to combat-ready status on the squadron. However, in due course the 'Boss' declares you combat-ready and you down the 'op pot'. After three years' hard work you are in the front line.

THE NAVIGATOR

Navigation is both an art and a science and, like other disciplines, must develop to meet changing environments and scenarios. The Tornado is now one of the most potent and capable aircraft within NATO and is likely to remain so for the next two decades at least. There have been suggestions recently that the term 'navigator' should give way to the American-styled 'Weapon System Operator' (WSO) as this more accurately reflects the tasks of, for example, the Tornado back-seater. Others have conjured up such terms as 'fightergator!'

In the fast-jet world, navigators are employed on the Tornado (strike/attack, recce and air defence), Phantom (air defence) and Buccaneer (maritime strike). As one would expect with a modern aircraft, Tornado is packed with computerized sensors for both navigation and weapons delivery. The back-

▲◄ Back in the Hawk again – but at the TWU, where the aim of the game is to get to grips with basic operational style flying and weaponry.

▲ Nose down and heading for low-level. Even though the forward view (from the back seat) is limited, the overall visibility from the Hawk is superior to that from many operational types, and there is plenty of sky to scan for the 'bad guys'!

28

seater can no longer be a navigator exclusively; rather, he takes on the mantle of a systems operator with responsibility not only for navigation but also for weapons selection, targeting, electronic warfare and mission-management. The computers are there to help him by reducing the workload of each task into a manageable whole. From that point on it is a question of the pilot and navigator working together, each with his own set of mission tasks, taking in information from the aircraft systems and outside references in order to achieve a successful outcome. This is no less true of the other FJ aircraft, all of which have received avionics upgrades to equip them for the early 1990s.

Although the majority of navigators leaving training are employed in the FJ world, there are a significant number of roles requiring such skills. All the operational multi-engine aircraft from the Nimrod maritime patrol aircraft to the E-3 Sentry airborne early warning aircraft employ navigators, as do most of the RAF's helicopters. The roles of the navigator in these areas are again many and varied and although in many instances he is employed in a traditional role, operational developments are leading to these crewmen becoming systems operators and mission managers as well. All start off in the same way.

▶ Into the aircraft, and run through the ejection seat checks. At TTTE all three user nations (the UK, Germany, Italy) provide staff and students and so you are quite likely to fly with one of your NATO counterparts.

▼ Classrooms and simulators (again), more facts and figures to learn, and more techniques to try out. With a complex aircraft such as the Tornado, the role of part-task trainers and simulators is even more essential.

All RAF navigators are trained at the Air Navigation School (ANS) of No 6 Flying Training School at RAF Finningley, which has been the home of navigator training since 1970. On arrival at Finningley, students join the BNTS (Basic Navigation Training Squadron), and straight away it is into the classroom for the initial ground school phase, covering such subjects as avionics, airmanship, guidance, meteorology and, of course, navigation. One of the first tasks of the last-mentioned subject is to prove to one and all that the Earth is not round but an 'oblate spheroid' (that is, its equatorial circumference is greater than its polar circumference) and that this causes problems when it comes to making a map – the basic tool of the navigator. Having completed weeks of theory, with a short break for four trips in a Bulldog as an introduction to flying, and learnt the basic rudiments of how to get from A to B, it is time to put theory into practice – but not as yet in an aircraft! It is simply not viable to undertake all training in the air, and so extensive use is made of simulators.

The main simulator is a block of cubicles each of which represents the navigator station in the aircraft, where the student can 'fly' around to practice the techniques and procedures just as in the real thing. In line with front-line

▲◀Gear on the way up just before the burners are cut. The Tornado is a truly amazing aircraft and the first few sorties are spent trying to get to grips with the complex aircraft systems and getting a feel for the handling and performance . . . and, of course, finding out about wings which move backwards and forwards! (T. Malcolm English)

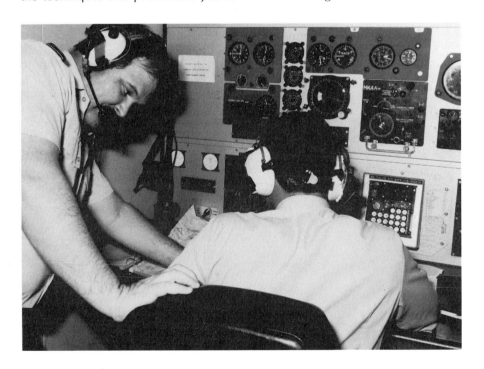

◀Nice try, but we are not actually there but here . . . ! The sim is a good place to iron out the bugs and resolve any confusion and misunderstanding.

▲At TWCU it is back to weapons and tactics. You know how to fly the Tornado – now learn how to fight it.

▲▶Operational on a front-line squadron after three years' hard work. The training however, never stops – every sortie is a training mission of one sort or another, from the routine low-level pair to the full-blown eight-ship on a NATO exercise. Plan, fly, debrief, learn – and do it even better the next time.

▼The Dominie still provides a sound environment for basic navigation training.

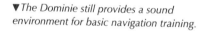

aircraft, the technique is a 'fix-the-kit, fly-the-kit' approach whereby the aircraft computer is used for sortie information. The trick is in keeping the computer accurate so that you can rely on the information it is giving (the GIGO principle – 'garbage in, garbage out'). To do this the navigator must 'fix' the computer's position in the real world using either radar or a ground beacon. Radar is a window on the real world in that no matter where you, or the computer, think you are, the radar shows you where you really are!

At last it is time to fly. The aircraft used is the Dominie, an adaptation of the HS.125 executive jet. In essence the BNTS course can be seen as a grounding in basic navigational techniques and airmanship as the student flies around the UK at 20,000ft trying to work out where he is and to find Finningley again. When the 55hr phase (half down the back and half in the front seat) is over he, or now she, moves on to the next stage of the course.

It is time for a complete change of style and emphasis as the student goes to the Low Level and Air Defence Training Squadron (LLADTS) for an introduction to two-seat low-level operations in the Jet Provost. Gone are the navigation aids and computers: now it is a matter of mental dead-reckoning

(MDR) and map-reading at 250ft. There is more ground schooling to cope with new ideas and techniques, but trainees quickly ease into the flying phase. Each sortie is tailored to introduce new elements, building up to provide a complex programme involving weather avoidance, fuel critical planning, tactical re-routing, low-level targeting and emergencies. The name of the game is flexibility – assess the situation and arrive at the best solution so as to achieve the aim, be that to put bombs on a target on time, take photos or drop supplies. After 20 hours' flying it's decision time – fast-jet or multi-engine? – taking into account the student's preference, the RAF's requirements and the results of the student's assessments.

For those destined for non-FJ aircraft it's back to the Dominie for another 21 weeks, giving 78 hours of flying and plenty of time to practise the traditional styles of navigation, including astro-navigation. Sorties are flown around the UK at 35,000ft and to overseas destinations to develop the flexibility that will be required for worldwide operations. For the FJ candidate it is also back to the Dominie, but this time with the Low Level Training Squadron (LLTS). This phase is very much oriented towards strike/attack, the aircraft being flown at 500ft and the nav using the radar and computer to plot a route and attack a target. This is all done without looking out of the window, thus simulating the night/bad weather situation. To develop capacity and flexibility an extra workload is introduced – a simulated engine fire and a diversion to a nearby airfield, worsening weather and consequent detours – and still the target has to be hit on time. And so it goes on. There are no prizes for missing the target or getting there late.

After 30 hours of Dominie flying it is back to the JP – and it is quite a relief to be able to see where you are going again! This final section of the course includes both strike/attack and air defence phases, designed to build on the previous training and also enable the instructors to assess capabilities and strengthen any weak areas. The posting decision takes in the same three factors as before, and then it is all over and the coveted navigator brevet is awarded.

A big sigh of relief and satisfaction, a party – and then it's on to another course! Eighty per cent of navigators follow the FJ route, passing to one of the

Tactical Weapons Units (TWUs) for more visual two-seat navigation plus basic tactics and weapons. This time it is in the Hawk, where sorties are flown at 420kt – a much more realistic operational speed. The Hawk is a superb low-level aircraft, and taking part in a four-ship SAP with another Hawk lurking around the route as a 'baddie' is great value. Having bunted around at anything between 4g and 7g for a few months and learnt that it's never safe to look inside the cockpit for more than a few seconds in case someone sneaks up behind you and chews your tail off, it's time to move on to the OCU. It is quite likely that the GR.1-destined nav will have met up with similarly routed pilots during the TWU phase and both will now follow the same route to the squadron and eventual combat readiness, as described above.

▲ *There are so many bits of kit to look at, the trick is knowing which one to believe and what to look at first. As a clue, the radar (at the bottom of the panel, in the middle) looks out of the aircraft at the ground and so must be telling the truth.*

OTHER CREWMEN

Almost all the non-FJ aircraft of the RAF – Nimrod, Hercules, VC.10, Chinook and others – employ air crew specialists in addition to pilots and navigators. The training for all these specialists is carried out by the Air Electronics, Engineer and Loadmaster School (AEELS) at Finningley, one of the busiest and most complex training establishments in the RAF. There are so many specializations that to cover them all would take a chapter in itself since the overall designations of the brevets often hide a multitude of sub-trades.

AEOps are destined for the Nimrod as either AEOp (Radar) or AEOp (Sonar); the former deals with such things as radio, radar and EW (electronic warfare) sensors – in other words the surface battle – whereas the Sonar man deals with underwater detection devices concerned with finding and tracking submarines. After a common basic phase, including flying in the Dominie, to cover basic airmanship and aircraft operations, students are streamed for their respective advanced courses. These take a detailed look at specific technical backgrounds and make extensive use of trainers and simulators to build a sound basic understanding prior to the student being posted to the Nimrod OCU. Air Engineer (AE) and Air Loadmaster (ALM) training follows a similar pattern, basic background academics on flying-related subjects being followed by role-orientated training. For the ALMs this means a move to one of the OCUs for the flying part of the course. In all respects these professionals contribute a vital element to the efficiency of the aircraft in which they operate.

▼ *Made it past the first major hurdle! Graduation time at 6 FTS for navigators and pilots (multi-engine).*

TACTICAL RECCE

ONE OF THE OLDEST of all military desires is that of knowing where the enemy is and what he is doing. To do this you must be able to see him! Over the centuries many techniques have been tried, and it was realized early on that the ability to watch from a greater height would enable the observer to see further. In simple terms this meant standing on a hill to see what was happening on the other side. The Chinese were the first to take this to its logical conclusion by imitating the birds and putting their reconnaissance into the air using man-lifting kites (possibly as early as 500 BC), but it was not until the late eighteenth century that the European powers, notably France, turned their attention to similar ideas – although in this case it was the development of the hot-air balloon which provided the impetus.

Despite successful trials throughout the 1800s it was not until the 1880s that the British Army had a true 'airborne observation' organization with trained Royal Engineer personnel employed in aerial reconnaissance, photography and signalling. Already the important facets of aerial recce had been identified. The limitations of the 'fixed balloon' were overcome with the arrival of the aeroplane, but the basic requirement of an airborne eye was simply transferred to the new medium and reconnaissance became the primary role for the infant Royal Flying Corps. The First World War brought a rapid appreciation of the value of this service: 'They have furnished me with the most complete and accurate information, which has been of incalculable value in the conduct of operations,' said Sir John French in September 1918. So important was the task that most of the efforts of fighter aircraft were directed towards supporting recce missions or denying recce to the enemy.

The small inter-war RAF had few resources to devote to pure reconnaissance but aerial observation was an important sub-role for the squadrons involved in 'policing' actions in Mesopotamia and India. However, it was during the Second World War that the true value of the art was once more apparent, and throughout the war visual and photo-recce proved essential to many air and ground operations. In the postwar period the basic principles have remained unchanged – obtain intelligence, both visual and photographic, and in the shortest possible time transmit that intelligence to where it is needed.

THE AIRCRAFT

One of the earliest successful collaborative projects, the Jaguar was developed by BAC and Dassault-Breguet to fulfil a requirement for an advanced trainer and close-support aircraft. Early in its development, however, it was decided that its likely potential would far outweigh these modest roles and it was redesigned as an all-weather attack aircraft. The Jaguar made its first flight in September 1968, although the first production GR.1 did not fly until October 1972. Entry into RAF service was with No 226 OCU at RAF Lossiemouth the following September, and this unit continues to operate the type.

The aircraft was originally powered by two Rolls-Royce-Turboméca Adour 102 augmented turbofans of 7,305lb (3,313kg) s.t., giving a top speed of

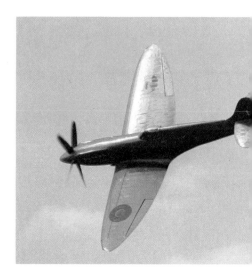

▲ *In its all-blue finish, the PR Spitfire looked a sleek machine. The performance of the Spitfire made it an ideal aircraft for the reconnaissance role, its speed making it all but immune to enemy fighter defences. A number of crucial intelligence breakthroughs were made by aircraft from the specialist PR units.*

▶▲▲ *Designed as an advanced trainer, the Jaguar exceeded its original specifications and was brought into service in the strike attack and tac-recce roles.*

▶▲ *Target details briefed by the GLO from the ATM and discussion of general requirements and intelligence considerations. If a target photograph already exists then this is used to help orientate the pilot.*

▶ *Target positions and task details to hand, the planning commences – plot the targets and work out attack tracks, bearing in mind photo requirements, sun position, defences, escape heading and a host of other factors.*

820mph at low level. The armament comprised two 30mm Aden guns, and external pylons for up to 10,000lb (4,536kg) of ordnance or stores were fitted. As with all modern combat aircraft, developments in engine technology have led to more power becoming available, the later standard Adour 104 being rated at 8,040lb (3,646kg) s.t. and giving an improved all-round performance.

The RAF, with eight squadrons (two recce and six strike/attack), and the French Air Force have been the major users of the Jaguar, but it has had a limited export success, involving sales to Oman, Nigeria and Ecuador and a licence-build deal with India.

THE MISSION

The biggest problem at the planning stage is to get time on the ground planning computer: briefing time is already fast approaching, and the team from the first mission are still working on the TABS (Total Avionics Briefing System). Nothing for it but to go and check on other details such as the tanker support.

The mission details are received from the GLO (Ground Liaison Officer) for a tactical recce of two point targets and a strip search. The standard procedure involves a pair of aircraft for this task, for tactical reasons of mutual protection and to ensure a back-up aircraft. However, the squadron is being heavily tasked and only one aircraft can be spared. With the basic details to hand the planning can start – plot the target positions and make a 'guesstimate' of mission time and TOT (time on target) confirmation. A quick check makes it obvious that tanker support will be required as two of the targets are in the extreme west of the operating area. The 'floorwalker' is informed of the tanker requirements for a tactical towline – its position and time and the fuel lift required. Back to the 1:50,000 scale maps to complete the planning of the IP-to-target runs, with numerous aspects to consider when choosing the ideal run

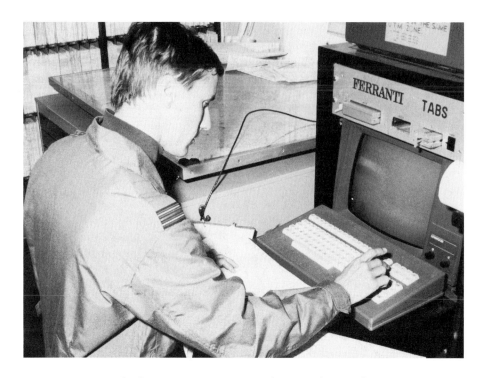

– target type and photo coverage required, tactical considerations (such as terrain-masking on the approach and known enemy defence sites), escape heading and many others.

The first target is a bridge and so care must be taken in selecting the line of approach to give the best view of the structure and its surrounding area. The second target is an electronics site which, intelligence reports have suggested, is being modified. The third target calls for even greater care with the planning as it involves a strip search of an area where it is suspected that POL (petrol, oil and lubricants) dumps are being built. This will require the use of the full range of sensors in the Jaguar's recce pod and the flight path of the aircraft must be planned in such a way that these sensors are kept over the target area to give maximum coverage.

With all the maps drawn up and a basic route decided upon, it is time to try to force a way on to the planning computer; fortunately, the previous team has just finished its recording – grab the seat quickly and start 'number crunching'! TABS is not essential as a mission can be planned by 'steam-driven' methods and details programmed into the aircraft manually, but it certainly makes the planning quicker (and perhaps more accurate) and eases the cockpit workload as the mission data are automatically transferred to the aircraft system. The system is 'user friendly', with on-screen messages providing prompts and helpful hints. Route data, using the map table, are stored as waypoints; IP and target positional data are inserted, along with the heights of these positions. With this information, and its memory of aircraft performance, the computer will calculate route details and present a graphic display of the route. Looks okay, so plug in the PODS (Pilot Op Data System) cassette and take a copy of the mission details – plus a hard copy print-out just in case! One hour from receipt of the mission and the planning is over – PODS cassette, target maps, route map, print-out. A final check with the GLO for an intelligence update – plot a newly notified missile site that is not far away from the inbound route – check out with squadron Ops, pick up flying clothing and out to the line to sign for the aircraft.

Whilst the planning was taking place, the squadron's engineering establishment was generating aircraft for the missions and ensuring that each had the correct equipment fit. The standard external fit for a TacR (tactical

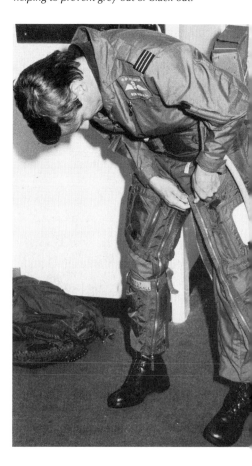

reconnaissance) mission is the recce pod on the aircraft centreline and fuel tanks on the inboard wing pylons; the outboard pylons are often configured with self-defence systems such as the Phimat chaff pod and the ALQ-101 jamming pod, essential survival aids in the battlefield scenario. The heart of the mission is obviously the recce pod with its horizon-to-horizon optical camera coverage and the British Aerospace 401 infra-red line scan (IRLS) system. The latter element gives the Jaguar its all-weather and night capability as the IRLS does not require light to expose its film. It is also of great use as a daytime sensor as it 'sees' into areas hidden from optical cameras (for example, woodland or camouflage) as well as providing additional intelligence by the differential heat patterns of a target.

A check through the appropriate Form 700 reveals that the aircraft for Mission 7261 carries the standard fit with no outboard stores. Time is pressing, with twenty minutes to planned take-off time – sign for the aircraft and walk out to the jet. Once around the outside of the aircraft and up into the cockpit; stow the maps and other bits and pieces out of the way, strap in, and run through the pre-start checks. The Jaguar's cockpit is quite reasonable in layout, not too tight a fit but also not over-generous on space – especially in full flying kit! Slot a blank tape in the cockpit voice recorder, check the camera controls and make sure that the 'mission notepad' (the 'Part C') is on the kneepad. Good – all set to go. Wind-up signal to the ground crew and hit the start switch to kick the Adour engines into life.

From now on you are in your own little world, with no-one to talk to other than yourself or the tape recorder. Silent procedures are in force so there is no need to make any calls to Air Traffic – just taxi out and take your turn on the runway . . . Brakes on, wind up the engines, brakes off . . . Into reheat – and away down the runway. Airborne, clean up the aircraft and climb away from

▼ *The aircraft is ready to go – fuel, weapons and cameras all set for the particular mission to be flown.*

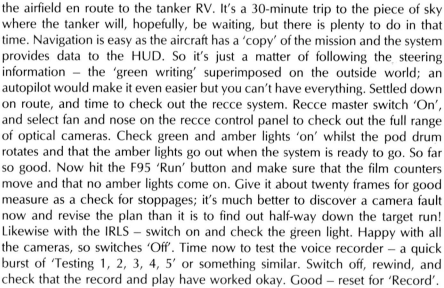

the airfield en route to the tanker RV. It's a 30-minute trip to the piece of sky where the tanker will, hopefully, be waiting, but there is plenty to do in that time. Navigation is easy as the aircraft has a 'copy' of the mission and the system provides data to the HUD. So it's just a matter of following the steering information – the 'green writing' superimposed on the outside world; an autopilot would make it even easier but you can't have everything. Settled down on route, and time to check out the recce system. Recce master switch 'On', and select fan and nose on the recce control panel to check out the full range of optical cameras. Check green and amber lights 'on' whilst the pod drum rotates and that the amber lights go out when the system is ready to go. So far so good. Now hit the F95 'Run' button and make sure that the film counters move and that no amber lights come on. Give it about twenty frames for good measure as a check for stoppages; it's much better to discover a camera fault now and revise the plan than it is to find out half-way down the target run! Likewise with the IRLS – switch on and check the green light. Happy with all the cameras, so switches 'Off'. Time now to test the voice recorder – a quick burst of 'Testing 1, 2, 3, 4, 5' or something similar. Switch off, rewind, and check that the record and play have worked okay. Good – reset for 'Record'.

The whole series of checks has taken no more than a few minutes and there is time to run through the rest of the mission to confirm that all is going as it should. Another look at the target maps, the route and the intelligence data, and sorting out the cockpit management – little things like making sure that the maps are stowed ready for use and the Part C is made out in skeleton form ready for the individual target details to be added. At the same time, there are vital routine tasks to perform – constantly monitoring the aircraft's instruments, navigation through the HUD and monitoring the other aircraft systems. And the most important task of all – 'lookout': there are no prizes for getting shot down, if you don't see the 'bad guy' then you don't stand a chance, and the fact that

▲▲◄ *Systems checked, and time to get airborne to meet the TOT for the first target. Tactical missions revolve around time – and the first aim is to get airborne on time.*

▲◄ *Canopy closed . . . final cockpit checks complete . . . green from the caravan . . . full power . . .*

▲ *Even with a full external fit, the Jaguar handles well at low-level. Outboard pylons carry an ECM pod (port) and a Phimat chaff pod (starboard), whilst the recce pod itself sits snugly under the fuselage. (Rick Brewell)*

this is meant to be 'friendly' territory is no guarantee of safety. There is a definite art to looking out of an aircraft for others and it needs constant practice to perfect. Every piece of the sky has to be scanned in a regular pattern, trying to pick up something that is slightly different – a small, dark speck that appears to be moving, a glint (was that a flash of sun on the canopy or wing of another aircraft?) . . .

With all these elements to think of, the time to the tanker RV soon passes. Now come the first tricky bits of the mission, first to find the tanker and then to make a successful 'prod' and get the required fuel. The position of the RV was

▶ *Gently does it on the approach to the basket. AAR calls for a delicate touch to make just the right contact and persuade the tanker to give up some of its fuel. (BAe)*

part of the mission data and so the aircraft nav system will take care of getting the Jaguar to the approximate area where the tanker is meant to be. After that it's a question of picking him up visually as the plan is for a 'silent procedures' air-to-air refuelling session. Twenty miles to go, 15,000ft – the briefed RV height – and the weather is perfect with just a scattering of cloud in an otherwise clear blue sky. So far the mission timing is fine but it's important to get the tanking completed in good time as there is not too much flexibility. Fifteen miles to go and time to start thinking about where the tanker is . . . Ten miles . . . Is that speck in the 1230 dirt on the canopy or an aircraft? It doesn't rub out with the back of a glove so it must be an aircraft! Now, is it the tanker or something else? Eight miles and the speck is bigger and seems to be sitting steadily in place. Yes, without doubt it's the tanker – right place and right time. Slow down a bit so as not to go rushing past and ease along the port side of the VC.10K so that the Captain can see that you have arrived and are ready for business.

The port wing hose starts to trail to acknowledge your presence and show which part of the 'petrol station' is open. Ease back a little and stabilize behind the refuelling basket . . . The probe is now extended above and to the right-hand side of the canopy and all other checks are complete. This part of the exercise calls for gentle handling of controls and throttles in an endeavour to stick the probe into the basket in just the right place and at the right speed to ensure a good contact. Too fast, and the hose will bend and possibly break; too

slow, and the fuel will flow around the probe and over the aircraft rather than down the probe and into the tanks! The procedure has been likened to trying to put a walking stick through a doughnut which is rolling down a hill! The trick is not to look at the basket but to concentrate on the known reference points on the tanker itself: looking at the basket can lead to a ballet of trying to chase the basket as it gyrates – interesting to watch but a fruitless exercise. All goes well – good contact and the fuel flows. The allotted fuel is soon taken aboard and the aircraft drops back; a silent farewell to the tanker and on with the mission. Airborne for 40 minutes and not far to go to the low-level let-down point.

The Jaguar cruises well at 250ft and 420kt; it is a stable aircraft and the control response is good. On the tactical side, another advantage is that it is a small aircraft and therefore harder to see. The route has been planned to avoid all known defence sites and to make the best use of terrain screening where possible. The HUD displays all the vital information in the standard 'green writing' as the aircraft hugs the contours of the ground. Time is shared between scanning the head-down displays, flying the HUD and 'lookout'. It's a regular cycle from one to the other, a cycle which practice has made second nature. All navigation systems degrade in accuracy over a period of time and the Jaguar FIN1064 digital nav/attack system is no different, although it is a reliable piece of kit. Time now to update the system from one of the pre-planned fixpoints.

Approaching the first IP, grab the target map and scan it once more, looking to pick up the IP of the edge of a group of distinctive lakes below a wooded hillside . . . From there heading 210 for a one-minute fifteen-second run to pass down the right-hand side of the bridge. Switch on the IRLS before the IP to give it time to cool down.

Over a set of pylons, a wooded hill just to the right, and there are the lakes as expected at the foot of the hill. A quick jink right to bring the aircraft over the IP and set off on the attack heading. Keep the 'lookout' going and navigate down the 1:50,000 scale map . . . 100 metres to the right of a church tower . . . clear of the village . . . track good, time good. IRLS confirmed running and ready to go with the fan of cameras. The next feature to look for is an isolated wooded hill which sticks up from the surrounding valley – an excellent feature as it shows up from a good distance and also shields the aircraft from the target. Round the corner of the hill . . . Twenty seconds to go . . . Vital now

▼ *Camera doors open, and a final check on the cameras pre-target.*

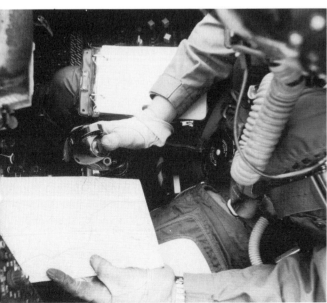

◄One target down and two to go . . . Check fuel . . . Plenty for the planned route, plus a bit in hand for any contingencies . . . Clearing burst on the cameras.

►The IP-to-target run planned on a 1:50,000 scale map to enable accurate visual navigation and lead-in features to assist in pinpointing the target. The plan is for the Jaguar to run down the left-hand side of the bridge, thus giving good camera coverage and enabling the pilot to view clearly the target for his Visrep. Having left the distinctive wooded IP, heading 218 degrees, the pilot aims to run down the left-hand side of the village at 20 seconds gone, avoiding overflight of the buildings by jinking left, then looking ahead to pick up the isolated hill at the 42 seconds mark and curving around its southern edge. Like most bridges, this will be a late show but the hill half a mile to the north and the pylons just short of the target will help to indicate the right area. Accuracy within feet now counts, and so individual buildings are used to enable a steady line-up to be achieved as the cameras are selected on . . . There's the river . . . follow it down. Just beyond that building should be the bridge . . . visual . . . A small jink and a good line-up . . .

to get the aircraft on the right line and stabilized ready for the pass by the target. The best clue is the pylon line 500 metres short of the target . . . Okay – visual with the target, so start describing it for the benefit of the tape recorder . . .

'. . . Road over river bridge, three spans, deck type, masonry abutments and concrete piles, one set of piles on a concrete island . . .' The easiest way to get the target in the right place on the film is to use the tip tank as a reference point: project the front of the tank along the base of the target and that puts the target in the bottom third of the frame on the film; it also keeps the target within the cover of the IRLS. Hit the event marker as the target goes past – the mark on the side of the film will help the interpreters back at base to sort out where the targets are on the film and so save valuable time. Off target . . . Cameras off, IRLS off. Clear of the target area and talk through the target in slower time, using the standard format for that target type as a guide. Add a weather report on the target area and which cameras the target will feature on. One down, two to go . . . Timings good, fuel plan about right, and there is plenty of film left.

The other two targets go equally smoothly although the weather is not so good in the area near the electronics. It is low-level all the way home but there is still plenty to do. The routine remains the same – craning the neck around, monitoring the aircraft, checking the nav system and flying the ground contours.

►►▲The Jaguar's recce pod, showing the range of optical cameras. The fan of F.95s gives reliable horizon-to-horizon cover whilst the IRLS provides the night/all weather option. The F.126 vertical camera is fitted for survey photography when required.

▼Although the critical points have been passed on the R/T, it is essential to get the film back to base and to the PIs as soon as possible. The aircraft touches down but the mission is far from over.

►►▼Brakes on, and the ground crew descend upon the pod to get at the film and rush it away to the debriefing area. The cameras are reloaded ready for the next mission.

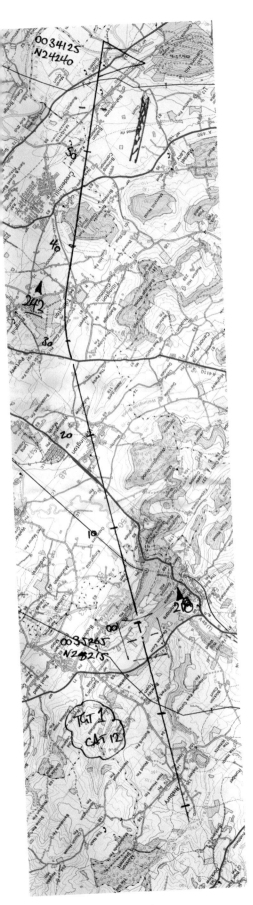

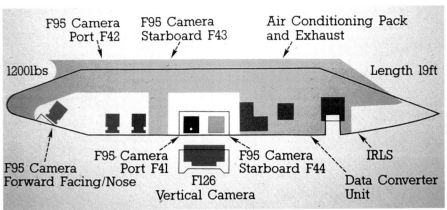

F95 Camera Port F42
F95 Camera Starboard F43
Air Conditioning Pack and Exhaust

1200lbs
Length 19ft

F95 Camera Port F41
F126 Vertical Camera
F95 Camera Starboard F44
IRLS
Data Converter Unit
F95 Camera Forward Facing/Nose

It is also time to tidy up the paperwork ready for the return to base and the debrief. The first thing is to give a good long clearance burst on all the cameras and then turn them off. It could well be that the tape from the voice recorder is all that the interpreters will have to go on if another mission is ready and no other pilot is available for it. Rewind the tape and go through it to edit the comments already made – add a bit here, correct a bit there – and make any general comments on the nav kit or cameras, problems or failures. The final item is to complete the Part C with basic target details, TOTs, weather reports and general comments.

Thirty minutes later the aircraft is taxying in to dispersal where a veritable clutch of ground crewmen wait to see to both the aircraft and the recce pod. The Jaguar has hardly stopped before the photographers get to work on the pod to download the film for despatch to the RIC (Reconnaissance Intelligence Centre); the clock is running from the time the aircraft's engines are shut down. All the target maps and the Part C go into a bag which is handed to the ground crew to accompany the film to the RIC. Within minutes the films arrive at the group of green cabins which make up the home of the PIs (Photographic Interpreters). The first stop is the processing cabin, and the films are booked in and are soon running through the machines.

Meanwhile the PI for the mission is examining the target maps and the Part C whilst he waits for the films to arrive 'on the table'. The still-warm rolls of film arrive and are fastened to the light table. Using the information from the pilot and the event markers, the PI searches for the target imagery. If not required for another mission straight away, the pilot will arrive at the cabin to give a

▲ Within minutes the films are processed and with the PIs for interpretation. Target shots are identified, written descriptions taken and checked against the pilot's Visrep and negatives marked for printing.

fuller debrief and assist with the target interpretation. The film confirms the basic details of the visual report, although extra detail is visible by carefully examining each sensor in turn; however, intelligence on areas just outside the sensor coverage relies on the pilot's input. Either way, the PI examines the imagery in order to provide the intelligence data needed, and the data are then sent in signal form to the taskers, and hard-copy prints are made and despatched as required. This up-to-the-minute intelligence is vital to the conduct of the battle.

FUTURE DEVELOPMENTS

In 1988 the only other Jaguar recce unit, No 2 Squadron at RAF Laarbruch in Germany, re-equipped with the reconnaissance version of the Tornado GR.1. It was not so much the introduction of a more up-to-date aircraft (and one with a better all-weather capability) that proved significant but rather the greatly superior reconnaissance system fitted to the new aircraft. The recce GR.1 was designed from the outset to maximize the all-weather/day-night capability of the aircraft and to that end the emphasis was placed on synthetic imagery 'to turn night into day' rather than on standard day cameras. The heart of the suite is the IRLS 4000 system which provides horizon-to-horizon cover with two SLIR (sideways-looking IR), providing extra resolution on the edges of the line-scanner spectrum. The system uses VCRs rather than 'wet' film and has a 'play' facility through the back-seater's VDUs for observation, marking and editing. The second Tornado recce squadron, No 13 at RAF Honington, received its first aircraft in the second half of 1989.

<table>
<tr><td>

Harrier GR.5

</td><td>

CLOSE AIR SUPPORT

</td></tr>
</table>

I N SEPTEMBER 1939 the German armed forces demonstrated to the world the devastating combination of air power and armoured forces – a combination which acquired the name *Blitzkrieg* (Lightning War). The use of aircraft in direct support of ground troops proved decisive. This basic concept of attacking ground forces with aircraft was not new: from the middle years of the First World War pilots had used their aircraft guns and hand-released bombs to attack the trenches. However, this was not formalized into a role of direct support until the latter stages of the war and even then it was a fairly haphazard system. The interwar years saw many of the RAF's units categorized as Army Co-operation squadrons; in India and the Middle East, combined operations were the norm, with aircraft operating in a variety of support roles. As aircraft became more specialized in the late 1930s so the RAF lost sight of the importance of the close-support role and at the outbreak of hostilities had no suitable aircraft – and, if truth be told, no real appreciation of the need for such an aircraft.

The German Stuka/Panzer combination swept resistance aside with the aircraft following the tenets of the definition of close air support (CAS) – 'Air action against hostile targets which are in close proximity to friendly forces and which require detailed integration of each air mission with the fire and movement of those forces'. The fire power and mobility of the aircraft were used to make an immediate and direct contribution to the land battle by breaking down points of resistance and so keeping the momentum going.

With the Allied ground forces unable to stem the flood of Panzers, it should have fallen to a tactical CAS aircraft to blunt the advance. Unfortunately

►*A Typhoon of No 193 Squadron in D-Day strip. The Typhoon was perhaps the classic CAS aircraft of the Second World War, having a rapid reaction time and a good weapon load, and its squadrons played a significant part in preventing German reinforcements from reaching the Normandy beaches.*

none was available. The Desert Air Force in 1941–42 became the exponents of the art of CAS in a theatre where mobility was the key. Existing aircraft, such as the Hurricane, were re-roled into CAS and given new weapons fits. More important still was the development of appropriate procedures and techniques, for example the need for close control of the aircraft, both to ensure maximum damage to the enemy and to prevent casualties amongst nearby friendly troops. By the end of the war the art had been perfected and it was common for the air controller with the troops to call down rocket strikes only yards from his own position. The many minor wars since 1945 have upheld the validity of air support, especially the CAS variety. The latest employment by the RAF of CAS was that by the Harriers in the Falklands War of 1982, the support of the assault on Goose Green being a classic action. During that conflict the Harriers of No 1 (Fighter) Squadron flew over 160 missions for the loss of only three aircraft.

THE AIRCRAFT

The Harrier is without doubt one of the boldest aircraft designs of all time. Its origins lie back in the 1950s with developments in jet engine technology of a high thrust-to-weight ratio, making the theory of a V/STOL (vertical/short take-off and landing) aircraft practicable. Of the many weird and wonderful designs, one showed promise – the P.1127. The concept was developed into the Kestrel aircraft, which was further developed into the Harrier. The GR.1 entered service in July 1969, optimized for the CAS role for which its diverse weapons capability was highly suited.

However, its primary advantage lay in its V/STOL performance – it did not need a concrete runway over a mile long and it could operate from semi-prepared strips close to the battle area, thus reducing reaction times and allowing for a greater sortie rate. The aircraft was an immediate success, but the development of its potential was slow. In due course the GR.3 emerged, with improved performance, a greater weapon load and a Ferranti LRMTS (laser ranger and marked-target seeker).

Development of the type may well have stopped there but for its adoption by the US Marine Corps as the AV-8A. This, plus the RAF's need for a follow-on CAS aircraft, provided the boost for joint development of the Harrier. With the introduction into service of the GR.5 in 1989, the capability of the Harrier has doubled both in weapon payload and operational range. The aircraft possesses a comprehensive avionics suite and the cockpit has been designed on the HOTAS (hands-on-throttle-and-stick) principle to aid system management. The weapons aiming system includes low-light TV and a laser spot tracker to enhance delivery accuracy. With its nine weapons stations the GR.5 can tote up to 9,200lb of stores in addition to its two 25mm Aden cannon. Two AIM-9L Sidewinder missiles and the very advanced Zeus jamming suite give the aircraft excellent self-defence capabilities.

THE MISSION

As soon as the aircraft has been pushed back into its hide under the trees the camouflage netting is pulled down over the entrance. Work begins immediately on getting the aircraft refuelled and re-armed for the next mission. Ground crewmen plug in the pressure refuelling system whilst the armourers wheel out the next load of BL.755 cluster bombs to be winched into position on the underwing pylons. Meanwhile the pilot has been connected to the squadron Ops by the telebrief link and is running through the debrief from the sortie just flown. This had been the first sortie of the day, and a pair of GR.5s had undertaken a CAS mission. The pair are already required for another mission and as the aircraft are being serviced the pilot stays in the cockpit to receive details of the new task.

▲ A demonstration of the flexibility of even small combat aircraft: Harrier GR.3s of No 1 Squadron en route to a winter deployment in Norway. One of the limitations of modern high-performance aircraft is their reliance on fixed, and vulnerable, main bases – a shortcoming which the V/STOL Harrier was designed to overcome. (BAe)

The Air Tasking Message (ATM) has been received by the squadron GLO as one of a number of requests for CAS missions in support of a defence link which is being hard pressed. Details of the ATM have to be checked against the general scenario within the squadron's operating area to confirm its suitability and to ensure that if the squadron is unable to meet the task a refusal message will be passed back up the line. With all in order, the planning can proceed – IP-to-target maps drawn, intelligence data plotted and crews and aircraft allocated by squadron Ops. The net result is that when the lead pilot of the pair checks in from Mission 1 he can expect to be called upon to fly another, invariably back into the same area (the battlefield situation tends to move fairly slowly) and almost straight away. ATM details are passed over the telebrief and IP and target positions copied down on to the 'half million' map. This map already carries all the essential area information, such as the all-important FLOT (Forward Line of Own Troops), and intelligence data on defended 'hot spots'. Being located so close to the battle area means that everything takes place very rapidly: there is no time for complex procedures and planning – as much as possible is kept 'standard' so that very little has to change from sortie to sortie.

AIR REQUEST/TASK MESSAGE

REVISED 1980

CLASSIFICATION NATO		DTG	
		INTERNAL COORDINATION	

PRECEDENCE				
ACTION:	INFO:		INFO:	
FROM:			MESSAGE INSTRUCTIONS TABULATE	
TO:			SIC	
			EXER / OPER:	

NOT FOR TRANSMISSION			
	A.1- AIR REQUEST TASK MISSION NO: 3 A 233		
A-2	A.2- [X] CAS [B] BATTLEFIELD INT [C] INT [D] COUNTER AIR		
	[E] RECCE [F] EW [G] ESCORT [H]		
A-3	A.3- [A] ARMED RECON [B] HARASS [C] NEUTR [X] DESTROY		[J] TEREC
	[E] JAM [F] DEF SUPP [G] CHAFF [H] SLAR		
A-4,5&6 TGT DETAIL	A.4- 10+ AFV AND TANKS IN AREA		
(PASS INFO IN FOLLOWING ORDER PER TGT)	ST 9551 AND/OR ST 9545		
- TGT / LINE NO	A.5-		
- LOCATION			
- DESCRIPTION/ CATEGORY	A.6-		
- CLASSIFICATION			

PRIORITY

B TOT	B-	Z [X] ASAP	NLT	Z
				[ ] NIL
C POSITION OF FRIENDLY TROOPS	C- FAC UPDATE		P	S
D.1 (INITIAL RADAR) C/S+FREQ	D.1-		P	S
D.2 (FWRD RADAR) C/S+FREQ	D.2-		P	S
D.3 (TACP/ASOC) CP+TAD/FREQ	D.3-	CP	P 291.5	S 257.8
D.4 (TACP/ALO) CP+TAD/FREQ	D.4- CP U 0017	CP U 0017	P 291.5	S 257.8
D.5 (TACP/FAC) TAD/FREQ	D.5-			
D.6 CP/OP/IP	D.6-			
D.7 MARKERS, SMOKE, PANEL. LASER FREQ, ETC	D.7-		P 291.5	S 257.8
E INFLIGHT REPORT	E-			
F SQUADRON/WING	F- 1(F) SQN			
G NO. AND TYPE AIRCRAFT	G- 2 X JAGUAR			
H SCL/SENSOR	H-			
J REMARKS E. G.: ALT TGT/ MSN SPT DATA/ REPS/AERIAL REFUEL DATA	J-			

CONTROL DETAIL

	ATC RULES APPLY EXERCISE	INITIALS	DRAFTER	TEL. NO.
COPIES TO:	R DTG			
COMM CTR ARMY [ ] ATTACK [ ]	C V D Z	INITIALS	RELEASER	TEL. NO.
CURRENT OPS RECCE [ ]	T DTG			
INT EW [ ]	R A N Z			(LOCAL REPRODUCTION AUTHORIZED)
OTHER [ ]				

AAFCE FORM 8001
(Replaces AAFCE Form 101)

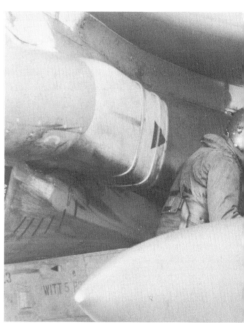

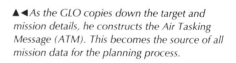

▲◄ As the GLO copies down the target and mission details, he constructs the Air Tasking Message (ATM). This becomes the source of all mission data for the planning process.

◄ Crew planning. A pairs mission, and both pilots examine the target map to determine IP, attack track and then many other factors which need to be taken into account. In the field, the pilots at readiness in their aircraft receive mission maps and details from the planning staff.

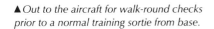
▲ Out to the aircraft for walk-round checks prior to a normal training sortie from base.

The GR.5 cockpit is roomy and comfortable, which is just as well because the pilot can expect to stay in the aircraft until he has completed, on average, six missions. Briefs and debriefs are conducted via the telebrief, and food, when available, consists of a sandwich box or the ubiquitous 'hot plate' of compo rations. Everything is counted in minutes. The ATM has called for a TOT ASAP (as soon as possible). Both pilots await the arrival of the target maps and hard copies of the ATM, which duly arrive by runner from Ops. With the basic plan complete, it is time to concentrate on the crucial part, the actual attack details and target run. The Litton inertial navigation system is programmed with the navigational and target data, final inter-aircraft briefings are made and the mission is ready to proceed.

A high-speed recce aircraft passing over the Harrier site would see little, the strip, landing pads and individual hides being made as inconspicuous as possible. It is important that this 'secrecy' be maintained to protect the site, and so take-offs and landings are made as expeditiously as possible. The camouflage netting at the entrance to the hide is withdrawn ready for the aircraft to taxi.

Operations from semi-prepared strips bring with them a major FOD (foreign object damage) problem, with a great deal of loose material just waiting to go down an aircraft intake. Emerging from their hides, the pair taxi towards the strip, flaps set to 'Cruise' and using minimum rpm, with nozzles at aft 10 degrees to reduce the FOD risk. The narrow, and not very long, strip has already been badly rutted by earlier use and so a rolling take-off is called for: roughly line up and slam the throttles to full power, with nozzles to 55 degrees. The 21,560lb (9,866kg) thrust of the single Pegasus Mk 105 creates a veritable storm of mud and debris around the aircraft, but the storm lessens as the aircraft lifts clear of the ground and climbs away from the surrounding trees. When the aircraft is

▲ *Fully armed and hidden in its camouflaged hide, a GR.5 waits for the summons to undertake a CAS mission. (Rick Brewell)*

◄*Maps and mission details received at the aircraft, final target planning and route considered – and it's time to check in with the other aircraft and get the mission under way.*

▶*A forest road provides an excellent strip for Harrier STO operations, and within minutes of engine start the aircraft is airborne and starting to climb clear of the trees. (BAe)*

▲ The GR.5 cockpit is designed for ease of pilot operation in a high-workload environment and uses the HOTAS principle to keep cockpit management simple. (BAe)

clear of these obstructions, the final transition into forward flight is made by easing the nozzle lever slowly forward. By now the No 2 is also airborne, and the important thing is to get the formation joined up as soon as possible for the short hop to the target area: ease off on the throttle to slow down, and jink to the right to enable the No 2 to join in battle on the port at the designated join-up point.

With only a 10-minute flight to the FLOT, there is not a great deal of time to get the act together and check through the mission data once more. There are two main items which grab the attention. Firstly, there is the standard tactical requirement of staying alive in a hostile environment – 'lookout', checking across to the area behind the No 2 (he will be doing the same for you). The 'sit-up' canopy of the GR.5 gives a superb 360-degree view, essential for survival in the modern air environment. Secondly, there is the need to get to the target area and deliver the weapons – accurate navigation to find and attack, with a single pass, a pinpoint target.

As the aircraft approaches the battle area the Zeus system is activated to take care of the threat from enemy ground systems. The heart of the system is the data processor unit, which has the job of analyzing incoming signals, comparing them with stored data and responding to any threats 'in an appropriate manner' using the active jammers or the chaff/flare pod. One of the unique elements of Zeus is the pilot/system interface which takes place via the aircraft's general-purpose display screen. Threat data can then be displayed in any one of a number of ways, including in the HUD and as an audio warning. As with any electronic warfare system, the problems come from the sheer volume of threat signals in the battle area: there is no time to sort out each one and so total reliance must be placed on the system to do its job.

The moving-map display shows the aircraft approaching the initial contact

point and it is time for the all-important call to the Forward Air Controller (FAC). The very nature of CAS work makes it essential that the attacking aircraft be in two-way contact with a FAC on the ground in the target area – his primary tasks are to update the aircraft on the target position and so bring about an accurate attack, and also to ensure the safety of friendly troops.

'Gladiator, Mission two-six-one-six on task'

'Roger Mission two-six-one-six . . . Uniform zero-zero-two . . . Zero-eight-five . . . Six-point-four . . . Nine tanks . . . East of small lake . . . Friendlies nil one thousand . . .'

In short bursts, the FAC has given all the target information from the IP to be used to the location details and type of target.

'Uniform zero-zero-two . . . Zero-eight-five . . . Six-point-four'

'Call leaving IP'

'Roger no additional info'

Speed 480kt, height 100ft – and scanning the '50,000' maps to note the details received from the FAC and take the pair towards the IP. Target details confirm those of the ATM and so the target position is in the INS. Not much in the way of features to look at between the IP and the target, but the small lake should show quite well.

'Mission two-six-one-six leaving IP'

The IP has been chosen as an easy-to-find feature from which to commence the attack run; the INS is working well and only a small correction is needed at the IP. Down to less than 100ft, and speed settled at around 500kt.

▶ *The major threat in the low-level environment comes from SAM and AAA systems, and the GR.5 carriers the Zeus countermeasures suite to deal with this problem. Zeus is an internal rather than a pod system, the only external evidence for it being numerous small bumps (as here on the wing-tip) around the aircraft.*

▶▶ *CAS, or throwing the aircraft at the ground, requires an exceptional forward view from the cockpit – as shown in this photograph. Even the supports for the HUD are as unobtrusive as possible.*

▼ *Although this trials fit consists of seven CBUs and two AIM-9Ls, a more usual operational load would be four CBUs on the underwing pylons, the AIM-9Ls, and twin gun pods on the fuselage undersides. (Hunting)*

There is no room for error and the navigation has to be spot-on to guarantee an accurate first-phase attack. The INS helps, but the basic technique is the same as ever with 'eyeballing' down the attack run and listening to the information being relayed by the FAC. As soon as he picks up the aircraft, the FAC provides a running commentary on target location and gives a ground description of the target area to bring the pilot's eyes on to the target. Laser marking is not available

▼*Climb up over the pylons . . . then back down the other side as quickly as possible. (BAe)*

for this target and so it is vital to acquire the target as soon as possible to settle the aircraft down for its bombing pass and get the best 'footprint' with the cluster bombs. This is grist to the mill for the GR.5: the aircraft has a rapid response to control inputs but stabilizes quickly and the HOTAS is superb, enabling 'switchery' to be accomplished in the least time and with the least effort.

Target acquired good and early – and in a vulnerable position in the open to one side of the lake. A perfect set-up for a cluster-bomb attack! No time to worry about the AAA (anti-aircraft artillery) and shoulder-launched IR missiles which all such units seem to have in abundance – speed, height and the self-defence suite will have to look after the aircraft whilst the attack goes in. There is always a good chance of getting away with a single high-speed, low-level pass, but anyone trying to go round again for a second pass, having 'woken up' the defences, is really asking for trouble. Try and lock the target into the ARBS (Angle Rate Bombing System) if there is time – it all helps the accuracy of the delivery. A good line up, and HUD indications coming down nicely . . . Hit the button, and the bombs eject from the underwing hardpoints . . . Jink away and get down even lower to clear the area. Retarded, the bombs fall away as the aircraft vanishes into the distance; the bomb casings part and the bomblets begin to spread out as they drop towards the target – each canister becoming 147 small munitions, every single one of which packs an armour-piercing punch. With one bomb giving a distribution footprint the size of a football pitch, the overall effect of the load dropped by the two Harriers is devastating.

Five seconds later the second Harrier has also cleared the target and both aircraft exit the area as low and fast as possible, rejoining in battle formation for the trip back to base. The final task before leaving the engagement area is to pass an IFRep (In-Flight Report) on the success or otherwise of the attack, plus any other useful intelligence or weather information. There is no time to relax – the flight to the field site lasts only 15 minutes but the airspace to be transited

▲ With the casing gone, the bomblets of the BL.755 begin to disperse, each one becoming a deadly weapon in its own right. (Hunting)

is full of ground threats, missiles and guns and there is always the danger of a fighter or two lurking; there is also the not inconsiderable danger of being blasted by your own side on the way back to friendly territory. All of this sharpens the awareness no end. It is certainly reassuring to have a pair of Sidewinders on each aircraft. The AIM-9L is without doubt the finest dog-fighting missile in the world, and any aircraft which carries just one of these missiles becomes an instant fighter, the missile making up for any lack of performance in its 'owner' – not that this is a problem for the Harrier!

It is a quiet trip home, the few ground threats encountered on route having been dealt with by the Zeus system. However, as predicted, the weather has deteriorated and the high ground to the south of the operating site is out in low

▲ Should the GR.5 need to defend itself against an airborne threat, it has Sidewinders to complement its outstanding turn performance. However, as a 'bomber' it is not meant to fight – the idea is to hit the ground targets – but it is never a bad thing to be able to look after yourself. (BAe)

▶ *The weather is sitting on the hills and so the pair have to sneak up the valley in 'fighting wing' formation. Keep the speed up, as you never know when you might be bounced!*

cloud. A quick glance at the moving map confirms that a valley just off track leads on to the lower ground near the site; the best bet is to try and sneak under the weather by making use of the valley. No 2 has already closed the gap between the aircraft as the visibility comes down, and to get the pair through the valley together he will tuck in behind and to the right, the machines manoeuvring as one. A jink off track puts the valley on the nose, and from this range it looks clear – the cloud is covering the hilltops and hanging down the sides of the valley . . . Move towards the left-hand side to give the No 2 a bit more room.

It is vital now to keep checking conditions ahead. Which way does the valley turn next? What if the cloud base comes down even more? Turn back or punch up through the cloud! Is there room enough for the No 2 . . .? According to the map the valley takes a 90 right and then starts to open up . . . Here comes

▼ *Now I know that the landing strip is down here somewhere . . . ! Finding the camouflaged site can be one of the trickiest parts of the mission. (BAe)*

the turn . . . The next part of the valley looks clear, so roll on the bank and round we go . . . Good – No 2 still in place. Cloud looks to be breaking up. As soon as the pair are clear of the valley and the weather permits, protective Battle is set up again.

The approach to home brings one of the biggest problems of the mission – finding the well-camouflaged field site amongst the rolling and wooded countryside. The squadron only established itself at the site a few days beforehand, and there has been no time for any local area recce to become familiar with the surrounding terrain, so the only way to play it is as a target run using an easily found IP to start the run in to the site. It is also important to start to decelerate from tactical speed to hover in good time! From the IP it's a case of track and time, plus a glance at the INS info, until, hopefully, the landing pad emerges under the aircraft in the anticipated place. With the Harrier decelerated into the hover and stabilized at around 100ft over the pad, the descent is controlled using the throttle – a most unusual experience. Back off the power and the aircraft descends, check the descent at 50ft to make sure that all looks good, then ease off the throttle again to settle down on to the pad, raising a cloud of dust in the process! With mainwheels on the ground, close the throttle. Back home! It is vital now to get off the pad and under cover as quickly as possible so that once more there is nothing for airborne prying eyes to see.

▼ *Back on the strip, and the idea now is to get clear and under cover of the trees as soon as possible. (BAe)*

Back in the hide the routine starts all over again. Ground crew swarm around the aircraft to get it ready for the next mission, and it's back on to telebrief to relay the debrief from this mission and pick up details of the next one . . .

FUTURE DEVELOPMENTS

The Harrier GR.5 will have replaced the GR.3 on a one-for-one basis in the UK and RAF Germany by the end of 1990, thus more than doubling the overall capability of the Harrier force. The 1990s are destined to see further development of this incredible aircraft, both with upgrades to the GR.5 and the introduction of the next variant, the GR.7 or so-called Night Harrier. Despite its obvious improvements over the GR.3, the GR.5 is still essentially a daytime bird and it is to fill the night hours that the GR.7 has been developed. The primary night vision aid will be a nose-mounted FLIR and a new HUD capable of displaying the FLIR data. A certain amount of cockpit reconfiguration will be required as the pilot will wear NVG (night vision goggles). Other changes include increased computing power and a new digital map presentation which also allows for the overlay of mission information. This will not be the end of Harrier development as the type has proved itself capable of adapting to the changing battlefield scenario through system updates. At long last the Harrier is displaying its true potential.

▼ *Almost as the brakes are applied, the ground crew start re-arming the aircraft ready for the next CAS mission. (Rick Brewell)*

STRIKE/ATTACK

T HE STRIKE/ATTACK AIRCRAFT is the descendant of the bomber aircraft in both its tactical and strategic applications in that it covers targets near to the battlefield and also those removed from it. There are many types of mission within the general category, from the CAS we have seen with the Harrier, through battlefield air interdiction (BAI), whereby the aircraft hits targets behind the battlefield – targets which have a direct bearing upon the battlefield (for example, reinforcement concentrations) – to attacks on targets deeper in enemy territory, such as airfields. It is the last, the so-called offensive counter-air (OCA) missions, which will be featured here.

The desire to destroy the enemy's air power on the ground was slow to develop as a tactical consideration. During the early years of the First World War, the Royal Flying Corps did not have the resources to spare for such a mission, although attacks were made on Zeppelin bases as these airships were used to attack the British Isles. Moreover, there was a general feeling that the air war belonged in the air and therefore the time to destroy aircraft was when they were airborne! It was not until the Second World War and the appreciation that air power was now a major factor on the battlefield that it was considered appropriate to try and destroy enemy aircraft at their home bases. Once again it was the *Luftwaffe* which pioneered the art during its campaigns in Poland and France. Bombing missions and hit-and-run fighter-bomber raids became commonplace, and even if aircraft were not actually destroyed on the ground the severe damage to installations and the airfield surface itself could prove decisive in limiting the enemy's ability to mount air operations from that base.

The lesson was hammered home throughout the war and survived the postwar revision of doctrine to become one of the major aspects of modern air power. Since 1945 there have been many instances of OCA being employed. During the 1956 Suez War, for example, it was considered essential that the Egyptian Air Force be destroyed on the ground before any further operations could take place. On many occasions the Israeli Air Force has shown the major advantages of wiping out enemy air power by destroying it on the ground. As the capability of aircraft to affect the outcome of a conflict increases, so too does the necessity to deny it any freedom of action.

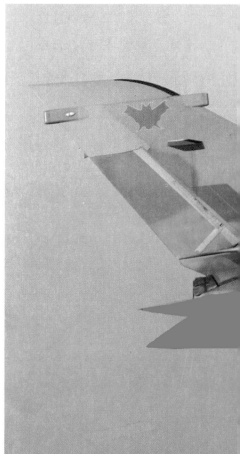

THE AIRCRAFT

Frustration over aircraft procurement during the 1960s led to the conclusion that the only way forward was in the direction of European collaboration on aircraft development, and the outcome was the formation of a European consortium to design and build a new NATO strike/attack fighter. By 1969 the consortium had settled down as a German/British/Italian group and Panavia Aircraft GmbH was established in order to produce the MRCA (Multi-Role Combat Aircraft). The design crystallized into a two-seat 'swing-wing' (variable-geometry) aircraft with advanced avionics to meet the range of roles required by the four launch customers – the German Air Force, the German Navy, the Royal Air Force and the Italian Air Force. The MRCA prototype, P.01, flew in August 1974 but it was

◀A Beaufighter of No 39 Squadron lets fly with RPs (rocket projectiles) at a power station in Yugoslavia, December 1944. The 'Beau' was a superbly flexible aircraft, performing a wide variety of roles, including the interdiction of targets deep behind enemy lines.

▼ The only items missing from these well-loaded Tornado GR.1s are the AIM-9L missiles on the inboard pylons. The aircraft carry eight 1,000lb bombs, plus Sky Shadow jamming pod and BOZ dispenser.

not until 1979 that the first true production standard Tornado (named as such in 1976) took to the air. Entry to service was via the unique Tri-National Tornado Training Establishment (TTTE) at RAF Cottesmore in July 1980, and squadron service began two years later when No IX Squadron became the first operational Tornado unit.

Powered by two RB.199 engines, each giving 16,000lb of thrust in reheat, the Tornado GR.1 has a top speed of around 800kt at low level. Whilst this is reasonably impressive in itself, it is not the main factor in the Tornado's capability; rather, this lies in the aircraft's ability to find and destroy pinpoint targets in any weather and at any time of day. Added to this is the extensive

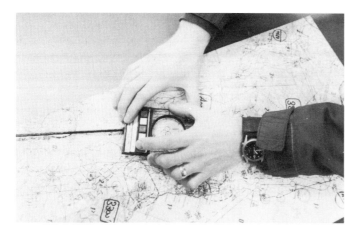

self-defence suite with which the Tornado is equipped to enable it to survive in the increasingly hostile low-level tactical environment.

The Tornado has, without doubt, become the most significant aircraft on the inventory of the European NATO air forces. Within the RAF it has replaced the Jaguar and Buccaneer in the overland strike/attack role, and it has also taken over from the venerable Vulcan. The RAF now operates nine squadrons of strike/attack Tornados in the UK and RAF Germany. Although replacing its predecessors on a one-for-one squadron basis, the Tornado has a capability which far exceeds this simple equation. At last the front line has a true all-weather, 24-hours-a-day aircraft which is capable of devastatingly accurate first-run attacks in a hostile EW environment.

THE MISSION

Having been dragged from an uncomfortable bed in the bowels of the PBF (Personnel Briefing Facility – the secure concrete structure which is 'home' to the air crew), you find time for a quick cup of coffee before the tasking signal is due at the squadron. Into the planning room to find out what number you are in the formation, so that you know what your particular set of jobs is going to be when the task arrives. Formation planning is, in theory, a well-ordered procedure, each member of each crew having a specific set of tasks depending on where he is in the formation – tasks which range from deciding on the route or target approach to making coffee for everyone else!

The task arrives – offensive counter-air (OCA) to destroy a fighter airfield, time on target being as soon as possible using four aircraft. The previously peaceful scene becomes chaotic. First, plot the target to see where it is; from

▶ A mean machine from the nose, with the 'eyes' of the 27mm cannon in the lower fuselage, the refuelling probe on the right-hand side and the laser ranger beneath the nose.

◄◄The CPGS map table is used to transfer route data into the computer: position the cross-hairs over the turning point or target, press the button, and the map coordinates are picked up.

◄With the route details in its memory, the CPGS will run a 'plan' of the route, giving time and fuel information. Take a copy on cassette and a 'hard' print-out, and planning is complete.

◄◄With any luck our aircraft will be in this HAS!

◄Load the cassette into the data recorder and check through the mission details on the TV/TABS.

then on teams can set to work on various aspects of the sortie. Pilots pore over the target area map to decide on the direction of the attack, the weapons, the type of delivery and such like – the all-important weapons–target matching. The aim of the mission is to destroy the fuel dump and control bunker as well as a SAM site on the airfield. Meanwhile the navigators start work on the route out to the target and back. There is frequent cross-checking to make sure that both ends are going to tie up! The target maps get copied while coordinates are calculated and the route is typed into the ground planning computer. Using the map table, a route can be transferred into the computer in a matter of minutes: additional mission information can then be added and the computer asked to provide a plan of the entire mission – times, fuel and so on. When the navs are satisfied that it all looks good and should work, it is time to take copies of the data on to a cassette tape for later transfer into the aircraft computers. It is also a good idea to take a hard copy of the information, just in case the tape doesn't work!

Into the briefing room for a time check and down to the nitty-gritty of the sortie. The lead nav briefs the route and the lead pilot the target and tactics. At the end of the briefing the four crews know everything they need to know to fly the mission and any one can take the lead should it be required. It is a true statement that a good sortie starts from a good brief, and with the tolerances that the formation are working to it is essential that everyone is fully in the picture. The time for questions is now and not on the attack run at 500kt, in cloud and just behind another aircraft.

A final check that no new intelligence has been received about the target or the route area, and it is time to go out to the HAS. Snug in its concrete house, the aircraft sits waiting, armed with four 1,000lb ballistic bombs, two AIM-9Ls, Sky Shadow and BOZ (a chaff/flare dispenser), plus a full load of ammunition for the Mauser cannon. There are no ALARM anti-radiation missiles on this aircraft, but two of the formation are carrying ALARM as well as the rest of the fit. A follow-up mission due on target a few minutes after yours is carrying the JP.233 airfield denial system. There is no time to waste as check-in time is not far away. A quick exchange of banter with the ground crew and the nav gets in to wind up the rear seat kit while the pilot does a quick walk-round check of the aircraft. The ground crew have already warmed up part of the navigation system by aligning the inertial nav (IN), so switch on the main computer and feed in the cassette tape with the route details – taking care to check that all the details are correct.

Both strapped in, canopy down and one engine running. Damn! A snag on the weapons system. Call for a technician to come and have a look, and keep your fingers crossed that it can be fixed. Luckily it is a simple snag that is soon remedied and the aircraft moves out of the HAS.

Time to taxi and to see if the other members of the formation are ready. One, two, three . . . Good – everyone appears to be on time. The aircraft moves into place on the runway for the take-off as two pairs, and still no word has been spoken on the radio. Lead gives the wind-up signal and the power increases from the one and two . . . reheat . . . combat power . . . and away down the runway. Twenty seconds later the second pair follow and soon all four are climbing away from the airfield and into the greying sky.

This is the boring bit – a 30-minute flight to the let-down point. Time to check through the route in the computer and make sure than everything is working as it should. Although part of a formation, each aircraft is its own little world, each crew capable of taking over the lead if required or going to the target on their own.

Time to go down, engage the TFR (terrain-following radar) and plunge into the layer of cloud. It's a mixed blessing as the radar emissions will give away

the aircraft to anyone listening out, but it is the only way to get down to low level through the cloud . . . 500ft, and at last the cloud layer breaks up. The radar is fearless: it doesn't think about the mountains which lurk in the gloom – all it knows is the height it has been told to go to. This can prove quite heart-stopping as the aircraft comes out of cloud in a valley with sheer rock walls climbing up into the cloud on either side.

However, safely down . . . and now the TFR can go back to standby so that the aircraft can run electronically silent. Time to get down and hide behind any folds in the ground – small valleys, hills, anything at all that will make the aircraft hard to see or track. Speed up to 450kt – and keep an eye on No 4, who is in battle on the port side, and scan ahead to pick up the other aircraft some distance ahead, sometimes catching a glimpse as they manoeuvre.

Approaching bandit country, and 80 per cent of the time is spent scanning the sky all around the formation but particularly in the six o'clock of your mate to check that no-one is sneaking up on him; he is doing the same for you. The rest of the time is spent monitoring the aircraft and the navigation, weapons and electronic warfare systems. Time to look at a pre-planned radar fixpoint to check that the nav kit is accurate. A quick squint at the radar to decipher the green blotches of ground returns . . . Use the hand control to move the fixing cross a bit – only a small error, so reject the fix and let the computer get on with it.

The Tornado's main computer is an amazing piece of kit and the general rule is that it knows better than you do most of the time – check it against the radar but be wary of moving its position too far. Unless it is having one of its very rare bad days (usually nav induced) it works to within feet and the data it feeds to the pilot's HUD are more than accurate enough to get the aircraft into the target area. A glance at the moving-map display in the centre of the nav panel and a confirming glance at the passing countryside give great confidence in the system.

Fix over, it's eyes back outside as the countryside flashes past.

'Felix 3 and 4, counter port. Bogey 9 o'clock, closing!'

In come the burners as the aircraft is wracked around in a tight turn to the left. Scan the sky and try and pick up the bogey as you strain against the sudden g force and the inflation of the g-suit, constricting the blood flow to the legs.

'Bogey 12 o'clock. It's a pair – two miles.'

'Tally.'

The counter has nullified the attackers' attempt to sneak up and the aircraft pass nose to nose. Now comes the tricky bit as it looks as though it's going into a turning fight. Get the head right round to watch what the opposition is up to, turning back in with a hard turn to starboard. As usual, it comes down to one-

▲◀Centreline pylons carry 1,000lb bombs: this is a fit with eight bombs on twin store carriers, but a more usual arrangement would be four bombs. Blue equals concrete – i.e., they don't go bang! (Paul Jackson)

▲Emerging from the HAS and looking for the lead aircraft to taxi by.

▼One of the formation, equipped with the JP.233 anti-airfield weapon.

► Reheats . . . and rolling. The aircraft vibrates under the power of the engines as the Tornado accelerates down the runway.

▼► Airborne, and climbing away in close formation. The pod on the starboard pylon is the very effective BOZ chaff-and-flare dispenser, the former to deal with enemy radar systems and the latter for protection against infra-red missiles. (Flt Lt Sommers-Cocks)

on-one, but you have to watch the whole fight to make sure that they don't both switch to you or try a sneaky shot as you pass the nose. The lead pair will have heard the calls and will have 'bustered' away from the fight as fast as they can to get to the target – the job of a bomber is to bomb the target, not get involved in a fight. This is not the best time to fight a Tornado, and the decision has to be taken to keep the bombs or ditch them: there is no point in holding on to the bombs if you are about to get shot down!

For some reason the fighters break off the engagement and run out in the opposite direction. Reverse and truck on towards the target a little puzzled. How much time and fuel has the combat cost? Can we make the target on time? Look

▼ *Both cockpits are roomy and well laid out. Although fly-by-wire, the Tornado has a conventional stick – as well as a manual reversion on the flying controls. (BAe)*

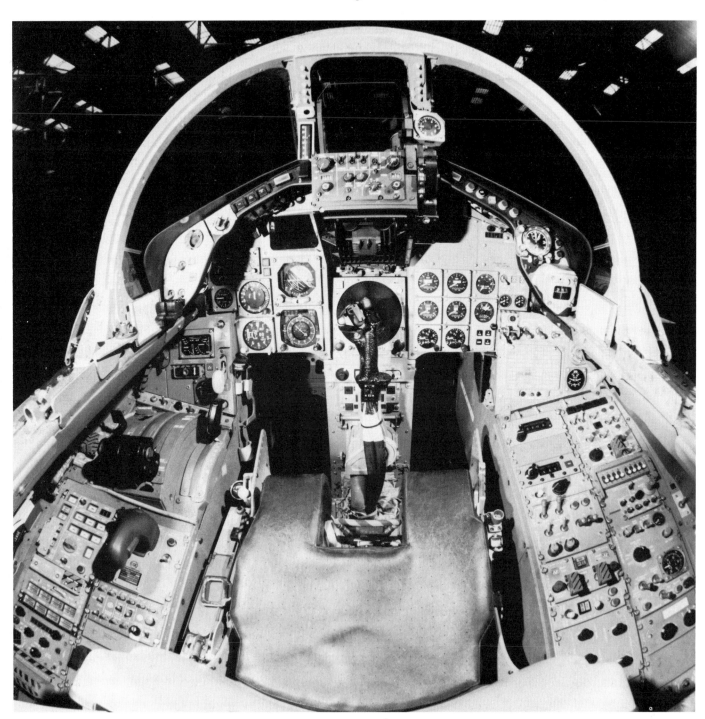

at the route, cut a corner here, fly a bit faster on that leg, and you can still get to the IP on time. Great! No sign of your mate, so for now you are on your own and all of a sudden you feel very exposed with no-one watching your tail.

Down at 100ft, the pilot concentrates on flying the aircraft over or around natural and man-made obstructions while the nav 'manages the mission'. The timing is good for the target and everything seems to be under control. Suddenly a more urgent note sounds in the earphones, the audio part of the radar warner, so glance inside at the display screen to work out what it is and where it is. A bit of judicious switching leads to the conclusion that it is a ZSU 23-4 'Gundish' radar in the 10 o'clock. This particular one seems to be no threat as it cannot

► *Wings back in 67 sweep, the aircraft breaks away to port to take up defensive battle prior to descending to low-level. (Flt Lt Sommers-Cocks)*

▼ *Approaching the target area . . . Wings back to 67 and speed up to 500kt plus.*

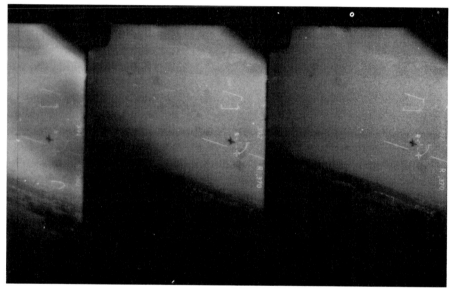

◄Level delivery: four 1,000lb bombs leave the aircraft and the retard parachutes deploy.

◄Sight on . . . In range . . . Growl in the earphones . . .

maintain radar lock and will therefore be unable to lay its guns on to the aircraft. No need to use any of the ECM (electronic countermeasures) kit, but keep a wary eye on it in case any of the associated systems are in the area. With its Marconi Sky Shadow jamming pod and the BOZ chaff/flare pod, the Tornado is able to look after itself well in the EW environment. The addition of the anti-radiation ALARM missile has made this capability even greater as the aircraft can now 'shut down' an enemy threat radar by launching a homing missile in his direction: even if it doesn't strike home it is sure to encourage the operator to switch off until you have gone past!

So far so good, but in 20 miles the route goes near an area which, intelligence reports suggest, may be being used as a build-up area for second-echelon units. It is amazing how many folds and creases there are in a seemingly flat landscape, and full advantage is taken of every one – the best way to avoid getting shot down is to avoid being seen, and the best jammer in the world is a few million tons of granite! The radar warner bursts into life with a confusing array of signals, far too difficult to sort out, so switch on the jammers, dump a bit of chaff and leg it away as fast and low as possible keeping your fingers crossed. Missile launch in the 4 o'clock! More chaff and manoeuvre, sink even closer to the ground as the trees flash past at 500kt.

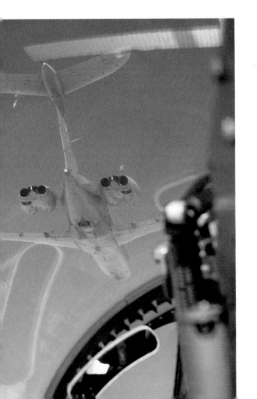

▲ . . . and the Sidewinder is eager to be away. Two AIM-9Ls give the Tornado an excellent self-defence capability. The aircraft is not a fighter but it can certainly look after itself.

▼ Operating range can be extended by whistling up a petrol station in the form of a VC.10 tanker.

Back to the job in hand, and time to check the accuracy of the computer again. Ten minutes to target, so into the target routine. Weapons selected and appropriate settings made. Keep the radar off until the last minute. It is now that the radar comes into its own – the 'kit' will give a bomb measured in less than 100ft, and by using the radar to give a final tweak the accuracy can be measured at a fraction of that; add the laser ranger into the equation, and the accuracy is second to none. The weather is getting worse! Low cloud and mist – good Tornado weather! Fifteen miles to target . . . A quick peek at an offset shows that the kit is good. Timing good, eight miles to go. Switch to the target . . . Not convinced, so bomb on the offset mark. Five miles to go . . . This is close enough, so light the burners, pull up, and throw the bombs into the target area. The aircraft leaps as the four 1,000lb bombs go sailing off towards the airfield. Roll over, get the nose down, cut out the burners and leg it the other way as quickly as possible.

Within seconds it is back to trees and granite flashing past on either side. Didn't see anyone else. No time to relax as you still have to get out of bandit country and back to base. With appreciably less fuel and no bombs, the aircraft goes like a greased weasel and turns like a fighter.

An uneventful trip towards the FEBA (Forward Edge of the Battle Area), and now only 20 miles to go. Was that a bleep from the radar warner? Maybe a fighter in the 9 o'clock? Scan the area. There he is – three miles and smoking in at a great rate of knots. Counter towards him to negate any missile shot. Now we can turn and the fight is on. Pull hard as he passes the nose, and keep the turn going as he has started to turn back in. Wings forward to tighten the turn, and radar into air-to-air mode. He looks to be on his own, but keep searching all around for any more unwelcome visitors. This one-on-one fight is developing into the standard circle, with each aircraft trying to close the circle and get a firing solution. Play the wing sweep and manoeuvre devices to gain a bit in the turn. Radar lock in range, Sidewinder growl as the missile acquires its prey. Commit (missile launch), and film the Phantom as it sits in the ranging circle.

No fuel left to play about, so off to the RV with the tanker to pick up a couple of thousand KGs of fuel before going to the weapons range to do a bit of bombing. AAR in the Tornado, as with any other aircraft, is an art – some pilots appear to be 'naturals', others have to work hard at it, and all have their own style with variations on the standard technique. Assistance, in the form of 'left a bit, right a bit' can come from the back-seater, who has a much better view of the line-up to the basket – a technique somewhat reminiscent of a TV gameshow of a few years back! With a healthier 'balance' in the fuel tanks, and all four aircraft re-united at the tanker, it's down again to low-level for the run-in to the range for an FRA.

Cleared 'Hot', and with the target squarely positioned under the radar cross, the aircraft settles at 200ft and 480kt for a laydown bombing run. Target visual and the gapped target bar sitting over the target – all other indications look good. Press the release button to confirm that you are happy with the set-up . . . The system will drop when all the parameters are met. 'Off target', and wait for the score from the range control . . . '6 at 12'. Six feet beyond the target – an excellent bomb by most standards but only average for a Tornado in this mode of attack. Twenty minutes later, the four-ship 'breaks' into the circuit for landing. Downwind . . . Checks complete and throttles rocked outboard to pre-select the thrust reversers and lift dump. As soon as the wheels hit the deck the spoilers deploy to kill all lift on the wings and the thrust reverser buckets motor to cover the engine exhausts . . . Slam the throttles forward and all the thrust is deflected by the thrust reverser buckets to slow the aircraft down. When a Tornado hits the ground with the intention of stopping short, it really does stop short!

It has been a good exercise. In many ways the easy part is over; now comes the analysis. Bombing scores will have been passed and the Phantom mates will be on the phone to discuss the results of the combats. Every part of the mission is looked at, films of HUD, radar and TV/TAB are examined and then the lessons are hoisted aboard for the next time. By the way, the range says that the missile got you – perhaps.

FUTURE DEVELOPMENTS

The future of the Tornado as the centrepiece of the NATO strike/attack force is assured for the next fifteen years at least. There can be no doubt that the aircraft has already made a significant contribution to the assets of NATO's air arm, and development programmes are in hand to ensure that it retains its pre-eminent place. Amongst these programmes, the Mid-Life Update (MLU) is the most significant as it will have far-reaching consequences in regard to aircraft and weapon-system performance.

The main elements to be incorporated in the planned GR.4 revolve around ways of making the aircraft more 'stealthy' and of allowing for an expansion in weapons capability. Passive sensors such as the SPARTAN terrain-referencing system, FLIR and NVG comprise the major changes to the navigation suite, although many of the existing systems will be retained. According to current plans, IOC is expected to be around 1993, GR.1s being upgraded to GR.4 standard. Whatever happens, the Tornado will remain a supreme exponent of its art.

▼ *With wings fully forward at 25 sweep and slats and flaps down, a GR.1 settles down on to the runway at the end of another comprehensive training sortie.*

AIR DEFENCE

E VERY SMALL BOY associates aircraft with one main thing – fighters! To generations it is the fighter aircraft which has represented the ultimate in military aviation (the same thing is still said by the fighter crews themselves!). In reality, however, air defence is a role which only developed in response to other air activity, and it developed in two specific ways. Firstly, there was the need to protect one's own aircraft from the enemy, and secondly, it was important to deny the enemy use of the airspace around the battlefield – a development dictated by the pre-eminent role of airborne reconnaissance.

The need to protect valuable, but vulnerable, assets by the use of escort fighters continued throughout the First World War, was almost ignored during the interwar period with the philosophy of 'the bomber will always get through' and rose to importance again during the Second World War – especially with the escort of bombing raids over Germany. The formal definition of air defence is the 'destruction of hostile airborne vehicles which threaten friendly forces and installations' – traditionally the destruction of bombers plus any escorting fighters which get in the way. In modern parlance this is referred to as Defensive Counter Air Operations – Active Air Defence Air Operations.

The origins of UK air defence lie in the need to combat bombing missions against Britain. In January 1915 the German airships L3 and L4 bombed targets in East Anglia; these raids were followed in May by the first raids on London itself. The public outcry was enormous and the Germans were jubilant, with headlines such as 'England no longer an island'. The British response was to establish an air defence network of fighters, searchlights and guns.

▶ *The classic fighter pair – the Spitfire and the Hurricane. Many of the principles of integrated air defence operations were developed by the RAF in the lead-up to and during the Battle of Britain, and these two aircraft had a profound influence on the development of fighter aircraft.*

69

After a difficult period during which new lessons had to be learned, the system proved successful and the Zeppelin threat ended. However, it was realized that a dedicated fighter organization was required, and this realization survived the postwar run-down. It is with the Second World War and classic conflicts such as the Battle of Britain that the air defence story comes into its own. The rationale for defending home territory comes from the twin desires of preventing attacks on industrial and civilian targets and protecting one's own air assets (in other words airfields). It is obvious, therefore, that an air defence organization (the fighter is only part of an integrated network) must react to developments in the threat it faces and where possible to try to 'second-guess' the opposition in order to stay one jump ahead. Since 1945 the RAF has had a string of classic fighters for this task – Meteor, Hunter, Javelin, Lightning, Phantom – each with its own unique set of abilities. The mantle is now being assumed by the latest in this line – the Tornado F.3.

THE AIRCRAFT

One of the British requirements from the collaborative Multi-Role Combat Aircraft (MRCA) established in the late 1960s was for a fighter/interceptor variant – a derivative which none of the other nations had requested. Development work on the so-called Air Defence Variant (ADV), to refine the basic airframe to suit the envisaged UK requirement, commenced at BAe in 1977. This involved relatively minor changes such as lengthening the nose to accommodate the Foxhunter air-to-air radar and provide underfuselage space for four semi-recessed radar-guided missiles.

The production of airframe components continued alongside that for the GR.1 and the Tornado ADV first took to the air on 27 October 1979. After a series of three prototypes to investigate aircraft handling and weapons release, production-standard F.2 aircraft were delivered to No 229 OCU at Coningsby at the end of 1984. The previous year work had commenced on the follow-on ADV, the F.3, which greatly improved the overall capability of the aircraft by using the enhanced Mk 104 version of the RB.199, a computer with a 128k memory, a second FIN1010 INS and two extra AIM-9L pylons. IOC of the new variant was with No 29 Squadron in 1987, and the F.3 is now the definitive interceptor Tornado, equipping all the operational units.

THE MISSION

'Merlin One and Two, to cockpit readiness'

The telebrief message creates a buzz of activity within the HASs, the crews climb into their cockpits . . . but there is little left to do as the Tornado F.3s have already been checked and are ready to go.

Since the morning met and situation briefs over two hours ago, each crew has sat in its HAS waiting. The navigators have entered the outline mission data into the aircraft computer, and the twin IN platforms, aligned by the ground crew before the air crew even arrived at the HAS, are stored with the aircraft's position to within just a few feet. Both crew have set their respective cockpits so that all that is required is for the engines to be started and the aircraft can be away in seconds. With its wings back at a full 67 degrees of sweep, the heavily armed Tornado looks a very purposeful machine as it sits in its protective shelter. The full weapons fit has been loaded – four Sky Flash radar-guided missiles under the fuselage and four AIM-9L Sidewinder infra-red missiles under the wings, two on each underwing pylon. In addition there is the single 27mm Mauser cannon – by no means a primary weapon of the F.3 but a useful asset should the fight get in really close.

Whilst the pilot is still getting into the cockpit the nav is already speaking on the telebrief:

▶ *The aircraft sits safely in its HAS, armed and ready to go at a moments notice.*

▼ *In the HAS control cabin next to their aircraft, the crew wait, fully kitted out . . . Time to take yet another run through one of the tactical plans. The call to scramble could come in minutes – or perhaps not for hours.*

▼ *These AIM-9L Sidewinder missiles form the potent short-range system employed by the Tornado (and most other Western combat aircraft). With their proven reliability and capability, they give the air crew great confidence in any turning fight.*

▶ Crew in – and a final check of the systems in both cockpits. Climbing the ladder in the full array of flying kit required for the modern fast jet can be quite tricky!

71

◄Even the two-sticker (trainer) versions are fully combat capable. Tornado cockpits are roomy and well laid out – important aspects for efficient cockpit management.

'Merlin One – cockpit ready.'

Within seconds the other aircraft also checks in, and both are ready to copy the task details.

'Vector zero-seven-zero, angels one-five. Contact Boulmer TAD four-two, back-up TAD three-seven. Scramble, scramble, scramble.'

No more information is needed to send the pair of Tornados on their way towards an intercept position – any other details can be relayed later by the ground controller at Boulmer.

Many things now happen at once. The ladders are removed and both RB.199s come to life as the previously silent HAS reverberates to the noise. A check that the helmet visors are down as the warning horn announces that the canopy is being closed. With the canopy down the noise of the engines recedes to almost nothing – the Tornado is a supremely quiet aircraft from the inside. As the HAS doors open the aircraft moves forward. From now on time is vital, and the aim is to get airborne as quickly as possible. Although most of the aircraft systems were checked beforehand there are still a number of vital checks on the weapon system which have to be made during the short taxi out to the runway. The Missile Management System (MMS) has already been put through its BITE (built-in test equipment) whereby it has carefully and methodically checked all aspects of its performance and has come up with a 'go'.

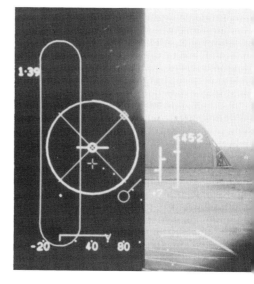

▲HAS doors moving . . . A quick run through the HUD modes to check symbology as the 'green writing' appears on the outside world.

In the back seat, it's time to check the all-important radar – select pulse-length, scale and scanner elevation, scan the pattern and check for ground returns to confirm that the radar is actually seeing something: a quick lock-on to one of the returns and a glance at the display screen for accurate information display confirm that the system is fully operational. Meanwhile the pilot will have checked the HUD and set up the standby sight. The final check is for the front-seater to take control of the radar by pressing the air-to-air override button on the stick and to confirm HUD symbology for Sky Flash, Sidewinder and gun in turn. To the practised hand and eye this takes but a few seconds to perform: the 'green writing' of the HUD is focused at infinity and the picture is scanned by the eye as the outside world continues to pass by.

With Merlin 2 in place on the left side of the runway both aircraft carry out engine checks . . . Full cold power and ready, 'thumbs-up' signal to the Leader . . . Select nozzles to 50 AJ . . . and a few seconds later release the brakes. The stubby orange flame of the reheat increases as the throttles are advanced to 85 per cent nozzle and the aircraft smoothly accelerates down the runway. Airborne, gear up . . . Flaps up at 215kt and out of reheat at 300kt

▲ Out of the HAS and waiting for the lead aircraft of the pair to taxi by. The large underwing fuel tanks appreciably increase the aircraft's range without greatly affecting its performance.

▶ Whilst not a primary weapon, the 27mm Mauser cannon in the lower right of the fuselage has a very effective close-range air-to-air capability.

▶ Clearance to go . . . Full power and burners in, the pair roll down the runway at the start of their mission.

with No 2 still sitting snugly in the 7 o'clock. Cloud base at 1,500ft, so stay in close formation to penetrate it; tops are reported as 4,000ft. As forecast, the aircraft pop out into a clear blue sky at 4,000ft, and beneath is a flat horizon of white cloud as far as the eye can see. Established on the briefed track and climbing towards 15,000ft, it is time to check-in with Boulmer. Merlin 2 breaks away to port to take up a protective battle position. It is never too early to get mutual cross-over going.

The ground controller confirms the position of the CAP (combat air patrol) but revises the CAP height to 7,000ft. By this time both aircraft are already going through 12,000ft, so level off and fly towards the task area at this height. Time to make sure that the 'office' is set up and to give the system another check. Using the other Tornado as a target the radar and weapons system are put through their paces once more and all looks good – symbology, indications, tone. The twin VDUs on the right-hand side of the rear cockpit are configured and the system data checked: the right-hand screen is set to 'plan', the Tactical Evaluation Display or 'god's-eye view', which gives an overall picture of the tactical situation in the chosen area. Using a data link from other aircraft, including AEW, and ground stations, the navigator can analyze a detailed and up-to-date

▼Airborne, and joined up before breaking out into protective battle formation. Mutual cross-cover is the name of the game: you look after my back and I'll look after yours. (BAe)

'Twenty starboard!' With a detection range in the order of 100 miles, the Foxhunter radar enables the crew to analyze raids and set up for the optimum attack well before engagement range. (BAe)

picture of all factors which might affect the mission. This, therefore, becomes a battle management tool, allowing the fighters to plan their tactics to suit the situation, although the general tactical plan will have been set out during the briefing in order to keep talk between the aircraft to a minimum. The left-hand screen is set to display radar data, not the 'raw' blips and assorted extras (most of it clutter of one sort or another) of the traditional radar screen but a clear synthetic presentation which has been sorted out by the computer!

With the pilot following the steering 'bug' in the HUD, there is no real navigation to do except for the occasional calling-up of a tacan or radar fixpoint to compare the system accuracy with an external reference – invariably the system is within feet and is best left alone . . . Fifteen minutes to run to the CAP position, so time to get down to the briefed height. No further word from the GCI and little to show on the TED – so far a very quiet day.

Approaching the designated CAP point. The plan is to set up a radar search pattern as GCI is unable to provide close control for this mission. You are on your own to acquire, track and kill targets and the pair must think and act as one to achieve success. The CAP is orientated as an oval race-track along the threat axis, each F.3 flying opposing legs of the track so that the 'up target' axis is under continual radar surveillance. This is no time for complacency, and not only must the VDUs be scanned for data but 'lookout', and especially the 'belly checks' in the turns at each end of the race-track, must be really sharp. The only prize for being bounced is to be on the wrong end of a missile.

With the F.3s established in the race-track and with pre-attack checks complete, the Foxhunter radar comes into its own. The main aim of the fighter is to kill the opposition without getting shot at in the process; with most 'bomber' aircraft only carrying short-range missiles for self-defence, the obvious solution is to hit the opposition at long range, well before you come into any missile envelope he might have. The combination of Foxhunter radar and Sky Flash missiles provides just such a service and makes the F.3 what it was designed to be – a long-range interceptor with a BVR (beyond visual range) kill capability. Gone is the old 'raw' radar picture – synthetic displays are the order of the day. With the radar set to the required search pattern, the multitude of black boxes within the system take the raw data received from targets, process them and display them on the radar VDU in the required format.

With the standard target search and acquisition display the VDU is uncluttered except for the data displayed around its edges – aircraft speed at

450kt and holding 7,000ft, plus details of the radar search area being covered. At last some custom: two plots appear on the screen as short vertical lines, now at 50 miles and 20,000ft but heading this way. No IFF (identification friend or foe) signal on either plot, and no friendlies expected in the area . . .

'Merlin starboard ten. Speed up. Two contacts 50 miles'

Move the marker out to the target blips using the hand controller, bracket the blip, insert, and the target is designated and given a letter. With both targets designated, switch to track-while-scan format to give a greater amount of information – each now has a vector line attached to it proportional to target ground speed and direction relative to the fighter. Chat within the cockpits increases as information is exchanged and displays are confirmed. There is no need to say anything to the other F.3 as pre-briefed procedures guarantee that each aircraft knows which of the hostile targets to deal with. Now is the time to make sure that the overall situation is favourable for the engagement – that no other targets have appeared that would prove to be a higher threat – and the set-up looks good. With the range rapidly closing, it is time to enter the selected target into the attack store to confirm it for attack and to call up the Sky Flash missile.

'Contact now 20 miles. Locking on. Looks like a good shot. In range. Clear fire.'

Meanwhile the radar will continue to track the other target. In the front seat the EHDD (head-down display) shows confirmation of the attack set up by the back-seater, the radar is locked to target A, and MRM (Sky Flash) is selected. As the range closes, transfer from the EHDD to the HUD and follow the steering cue. Target data and own weapon parameters are displayed, but in simple terms it's just a case of keeping the dot in the circle until the firing parameters are achieved.

'Fox One'.

The Sky Flash has been launched and within milliseconds of being ejected clear of the aircraft streaks off towards its distant target. It is important now to keep illuminating the target with the radar as the missile requires guidance; this is the worst part as it might bring you into range of the opposition's own missiles.

▶ *Up to the tanker to refuel before dropping back down to the CAP position. With AAR, the patrol time of the F.3 is limited only by the weapon load and crew fatigue. (BAe)*

▼ *Sky Flash launch. With its semi-active guidance system, this medium-range missile is able to engage targets under BVR criteria – well before the short-range self-defence missiles of most attack aircraft could be brought into play. (BAe)*

▼ *Wings forward, and pull around the corner to close for a Sidewinder shot.*

However, once on its way the Sky Flash has a very high PK (probability of a kill) and its warhead with radar proximity fuzing is devastating. Success is confirmed by the explosion to the right and way above – one target vanishes from the display. Seconds later the other target is also killed as Merlin 2's missile finds its mark. This is how it should work – find, track and destroy, and don't get involved in a fight. Engagement over, so get back to the CAP position and set up the race-track again.

An uneventful hour of going round and round, with no more radar contacts other than friendlies. A tactical towline has been arranged for AAR, and with fuel reaching the pre-planned 'bingo' it's time to go off to the tanker. Leaving the CAP point now and climbing towards 15,000ft, with ten minutes to tanker RV but no time to relax: the VDUs must still be analyzed as situations change rapidly, eyes must be 'out of the cockpit' for the maximum amount of time, and the navigation system must be checked after its three hours over the sea. Tornado is a very comfortable aircraft, but any ejection seats get hard on the rear end and back after a period of time, and other than loosening the straps and trying to stretch there is nothing that can be done about it! The ground controller can spare time to point you towards the tanker although the TED is already showing its position. The plan is to top up with fuel and get back on station at the CAP as soon as possible.

The TriStar tanker is ready and waiting with its hose trailed under the fuselage. Select 'Probe out' and set fuel switches for receiving . . . position behind the basket and move in . . . a gentle push . . . in goes the hose, and fuel begins to flow. All too easy – but then it is daylight and the air is smooth. It's a different game on a dark, dank night with the basket bouncing around in turbulence! With tanks full, it is time to move out and let Merlin 2 have his share.

Two hours later and another missile less – a successful attack on another high-flying target. Merlin 2 picks up a low-level raid at 30 miles – four aircraft in card formation. In with the burners and turn towards an intercept position. Once again the plan is to take out as many as possible with long-range shots but it is quite likely that one or two will get in close. Targets designated, tracking

. . . Select and enter into attack store . . . Symbology good . . . Sky Flash launched. One down, three to go. Radar shows ten miles, locked to target C . . . 6 miles . . . Visual with a pair in the 2 o'clock but no sign of No 3. With Merlin 2 swept out to port, turn in towards the hostiles as the range closes to three miles. Too late for a Sky Flash shot so change to Sidewinder. Although not designed for 'in-fighting', the Tornado has proved itself able to turn with the best of them and this, along with the all-aspect lethality of the AIM-9L, means that turning fights are no problem. With 'Lima' (SRM) selected, the HUD display provides all the necessary data to enable an early lock and so get the first shot away. Symbology good and seeker head locked on, good solid growl in the earphones and pull the trigger . . . The right-hand man has made the mistake of plugging in his burners, thus giving the Sidewinder the best possible target. Counter starboard as the third aircraft appears to the right of the formation but keep an eye on the other to make sure what he is doing – is he bugging out or will he turn back into the fight?

◄At the end of a long mission the sight of the runway is a welcome one.

With wings swept forward and manoeuvres dropped, the Tornado has an excellent instant turn capability to negate a shot or to create a shooting opportunity. Once around, back with the wings to build up energy once more to continue the fight. Formation integrity is still good, and there is no sign of the other opponents. The fight is now down to below 1,000ft, and a call for a counter port means the loss of the aircraft on the nose. Reverse – and the sky is empty! Like all combats, this one is over suddenly – one minute the fight is on and the next there is nobody there! As pre-arranged, the mission will meet up again at the CAP point. Both aircraft arrive at around the same time and set up yet another race-track. Not long to go as the next pair are due on task soon.

The transit home is uneventful, and after a five-hour mission the sight of the airfield is most welcome. Break into the circuit . . . Downwind . . . Pre-landing checks . . . Arm the lift dump and thrust-reverser systems by 'rocking' the throttles outboard. Round final . . . Speed coming back . . . Wheels hit the tarmac and the spoilers pop up on the wings to kill the lift. The buckets of the thrust reverser system close over the engine nozzles . . . Slam the throttles forward (a most unnatural action at a time when you want to stop the aircraft) and the power of the RB.199s is used to slow the aircraft to a walking pace . . . Happy, so select 'buckets in' and taxi off the runway. Before long the aircraft is back in the HAS where the whole routine will start again. An aircraft without fuel and weapons is a waste: by the time the debrief is under way the two F.3s will be ready to go again and other crews will be sitting in the HASs.

FUTURE DEVELOPMENTS

By late 1990 the last of the planned Tornado F.3 squadrons will have formed with the completion of re-equipment of the Leuchars Wing. One of the major advantages of a software-orientated system is that as long as the basic airframe is usable then the capability can be upgraded or modified to suit changing needs. The net result is that the Tornado F.3 should have a long career and be the subject of various upgrades – the aircraft may, for example, receive the next generation of air-to-air missiles, AMRAAM (Advanced Medium-Range AAM) and ASRAAM (Advanced Short-Range AAM). Outline planning has commenced for a mid-life update (MLU), although no specific details are yet available.

◄An aircraft sitting in the open on an airfield is too good a target and so the Tornado must be winched back into its HAS as quickly as possible, protected and made ready for the next mission.

►Planned improvement programmes for the F.3 include a new generation of missiles such as AMRAAM, a fire-and-forget BVR weapon which will greatly increase the engagement capability of the aircraft, and ASRAAM, an improved 'dogfighting' missile. (BAe)

TACTICAL SUPPORT

Chinook

OF ALL THE ROLES examined in this book, that of the tactical helicopter is the most recently introduced, having a history of less than 40 years. Tactical support arose as a secondary consideration to the original concept for the operational employment of the helicopter. Helicopter development was slow and uncertain in the mid-1940s, although the RAF did operate a small number of Sikorsky VS-316s, known as Hoverfly Is in British service. The follow-on helicopter, the Hoverfly II, came from the same stable, but despite these early trials there was a distinct lack of enthusiasm for the potential of the new aircraft type. Nevertheless, a requirement was identified for various helicopter types to cover a wide range of duties, although in practice the RAF received one type – the Westland Dragonfly, a licence-built version of the Sikorsky S-51, which entered service in 1950. The same year the FEAF Casualty Evacuation Flight was formed and the true value of helicopters began to be appreciated. Dragonfly (and later Sycamore) operations in the Far East convinced most of the doubters that this element was worthy of expansion.

The potential of the helicopter in the tactical roles of troop and supply movement were clearly demonstrated by the Dragonfly and Sycamore operations, but what was needed was a helicopter capable of lifting more and going further. Development work on an aircraft to meet this early 1950s requirement led to the Bristol Belvedere, a twin-rotor, twin-engine design capable of lifting 25 troops (short range) or a 6,000lb load. The first squadron, No 66, did not form, however, until September 1961: the aircraft had had a troubled development period and came close to cancellation on a number of occasions. It likewise had a troubled service life.

Three squadrons operated the Belvedere, and in the Far East it did a superb job, despite numerous problems, between 1961 and 1969, proving invaluable during the troubles in Brunei in the mid-1960s. In the Middle East, however, with operations in Aden, it struggled against even greater odds and, despite once more proving invaluable for the rapid deployment of troops, never truly established itself.

The Belvedere had certainly proved that an aircraft of its type was vital in the tactical support role and as the problems mounted and it neared the end of its useful life a requirement was written for a replacement. Amongst the contenders was the Boeing Vertol CH-47 Chinook, and the intention was for the new type to enter service in 1970. However, for a variety of reasons nothing came of this and the project, and the Chinook, were abandoned in favour of smaller tactical helicopters – a change of emphasis which led to the development and entry into service of the Puma.

THE AIRCRAFT

Ten years later the requirement for a heavy-lift helicopter emerged once more, and this time there were no British-built contenders and the obvious choice was the latest version of the previously rejected Chinook! The prototype YCH-47A had first flown in September 1961 and entered service shortly afterwards, seeing

▶ *The distinctive shape of the twin-rotor Chinook carrying a somewhat unusual underslung load, a Polish MiG, to the Finningley Air Show. With its 20,000lb payload, the Chinook introduced a new dimension to RAF helicopter support capabilities.*

▼ *The RAF's original heavy-lift helicopter was the Belvedere; one is seen here re-supplying a remote mountain outpost in Aden. Without such missions, the ground forces' task of monitoring and controlling huge expanses of inhospitable terrain would have been almost impossible.*

▼▶ *Planning must take account of all factors and make use of the aircraft's ability to hide from unfriendly eyes by 'nap-of-the-Earth' flying.*

extensive service over the next ten years in Vietnam where it revealed its flexibility and potential. Development of the type continued, with new variants appearing and an ever-growing list of customers. The resurgence of interest in the late 1970s included that of the RAF, and the first Chinooks (roughly equivalent to the CH-47C variant) went to No 240 OCU at Odiham in 1980 and to the first squadron the following year.

With its two 3,750shp Lycoming T-55-L-11 turboshafts (updated to T-55-L712E in 1983–84), the Chinook has a maximum speed of 160kt, although the more normal cruising speed is 120kt. The aircraft is capable of taking a load in excess of 22,000lb, thus making a significant contribution to battlefield support in a variety of forms. During the Falklands conflict the single operational Chinook performed outstandingly well, lifting, on one occasion, 86 combat troops.

THE MISSION

The eight-figure grid reference plots out to be a reasonably sized clearing in an area of woodland – a fairly typical Landing Zone (LZ) for a battlefield support mission. Details of the loads to be moved and the location of the FEBA (Forward Edge of the Battle Area) should be received shortly, but in the meantime the Task Leader has to parcel out tasks to the remainder of the crews in the formation. At first sight it looks as though three or four Chinooks will be needed.

The detachment has been operating from its field site alongside the Army unit for five days, and coordination between the two is well established. With the majority of the equipment camouflaged on the edge of the operating site, it is only the helicopters themselves which give away the location – one of the problems with the Chinook is that it is too large to push away under the trees and cover with netting. However, the flying rate is high and the aircraft are rarely on the ground; both day and night missions are flown, the latter using NVGs. Support elements are present with the TSW (Tactical Supply Wing), providing the refuelling facilities with bowsers and pillow tanks, and squadron ground crew to service the aircraft whilst at the main base; at outlying stations the crew themselves carry out the aircraft servicing.

With the LZ plotted the other questions now have to be answered. What troops and equipment have to be moved? Is it better to shuttle the troops or re-rig the aircraft for maximum capacity? What other loads are involved? Can

mixed loads be used? Will the aircraft need to refuel? And – vitally important – what is the battlefield situation and therefore what tactics will have to be employed? A host of points to consider before the aircraft can carry out the task, so there is plenty for the crew to sort out. The Army commander briefs the Task Leader on the requirements and general situation – a mixed force of troops and equipment, including heavy loads that will require underslung movement. The LZ is some 30 minutes' flying time away and right on the edge of the battle area; the deployment is intended as a concealed build-up. However, the LZ has been secured by a ground party and a group from MAOT (Mobile Air Operations Team) will have marked out the LZ and will act as aircraft coordinators. Despite the high air threat (including armed helicopters) in the task area, no armed escort helicopters can be provided – the Chinooks will have to rely on their own door-mounted GPMGs (general-purpose machine guns) to suppress any ground fire in the LZ area.

Details of the loads are examined and aircraft loading decided upon . . . Four aircraft should be enough for the first wave, with a second, similar wave following later – two aircraft to take troops, one with vehicle and troops, and one with the underslung loads. The troop-carrying aircraft will go first in the

▲◄Two front crewmen check out the aircraft systems and avionics whilst the two down the back stow any equipment and ensure that the cabin is rigged for the planned load. The spacious cabin of the Chinook has been kept simple to allow for flexibility in taking aboard internal loads.

▼◄The sides and rear of the aircraft are blind spots for the pilots, so the crewmen act as the 'eyes', ensuring that the aircraft is safe to manoeuvre.

formation as their 'cargo' will be useful in helping to secure the LZ should any problems arise. In view of the overall situation the Chinooks will fly NOE (nap-of-the-Earth), hugging the contours, and plan a CAD (concealed approach and departure) run-in to the LZ itself. The idea is to get in and out without alerting the opposition and without giving away the exact location of the LZ.

The brief to the troops is short and sharp as they have all flown 'Chinook Airways' before and know the procedures and what to expect. The crewmen, two per aircraft, have prepared the cabins for their respective loads, and as the time ticks away loading must be smooth and efficient. In two lines, the 26 troops move into the body of the Chinook to take up the seats which run down both sides; the other aircraft has a greater complement of troops and so the floor seating is also brought into use. With their standard equipment, including rucksacks, the cabin appears full. Time is of the essence now . . .

'Fifteen troops to go. Expect take-off in two minutes'.

The running commentary by the crewmen keeps the front-end pilots informed of the progress of the loading. The engines are running and the Chinook is ready to go . . .

'Ramp up. Troops secure. You are clear above and behind.'

With the two crewmen watching front and back – the 'eyes' of the pilots who cannot see to the sides and rear of the aircraft – the Chinook lifts up and as it clears all obstacles translates to forward flight. The second troop-carrying helicopter lifts off at almost the same instant, and seconds later the third Chinook is airborne, the loading of the vehicle having gone smoothly since it was already prepared for flight and the driver had played the 'quart into a pint pot' driving game before. Meanwhile the aircraft with the underslung load is manoeuvring for the final pick-up. Again, the role of the crewmen is essential: the directions from one crewman position the helicopter just about over the load, and these are then taken up by the other as he peers down through the floor hatch . . .

'Forward ten and right . . . Forward only . . . Forward . . . Five . . . four . . . three . . . Forward two . . . one . . . Steady . . . Steady . . . Height good, position good.'

Stabilized over the load, the pilot looks for external references to maintain his position whilst the running commentary from the back continues . . .

'Load attached . . . Up gently . . . Taking the strain . . . Load clear of the ground . . . Good load . . .'

The Chinook has an incredible amount of power in its twin engines and even by doubling its overall weight, as it often does with such loads, it handles

◀ With the side-seating prepared, the two lines of troops move into the aircraft to take up their positions. Additional seating can be rigged on the floor, almost doubling the troop capacity.

smoothly and accurately. Nevertheless, the effect of the great weight under the aircraft can be felt – especially during turns or if the load starts to oscillate. Slightly behind the other aircraft, No 4 departs the clearing and sets off towards the LZ.

A passing glance over the undulating and partly wooded landscape would reveal nothing – the Chinooks seem to blend with the background at 120kt and

▼ Within minutes, loading is complete and the aircraft lifts off.

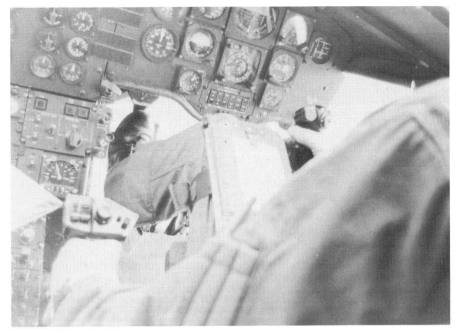

► *Despite its size and seemingly cumbersome shape, the Chinook is highly manouevrable. One pilot flies the aircraft whilst the other looks after the map-reading.*

▼ *From the side door, the crewman glances at his map as a cross-check on the navigation . . . but most of his time is spent scanning the horizon for aircraft – see it, call it and assess the probability of a threat.*

less than 100ft. A slow speed has two great advantages in that you can navigate by smaller features and search out every possible hiding place, and the movement over the ground is slow enough not to register with the casual observer. The planned route on the map aims at avoiding all problem areas, but the basic concept is to avoid being seen by anyone – if they don't see you then they won't fire at you! The handling pilot's job is to keep the aircraft in the NOE environment – wriggle down a small valley, sneak around the edge of a ridge, even duck down behind a line of woods. Meanwhile the other pilot, or nav, concentrates on map-reading, keeping to rough track and time to avoid known hazards and make the LZ as planned.

'See that wood on the ridge in the ten o'clock? Put me down the left-hand side!'

With the general direction fixed, the aircraft manoeuvres around to seek the best ground cover; even such gentle manoeuvres can be very uncomfortable for the troops down the back. Although navigation is the prime task of one of the pilots, it cannot become his sole task – there just is not time to spare – and so a nav computer, the TANS (Tactical Air Navigation System) is employed to help reduce the nav workload. Programmed with a series of waypoints (turning points), the system provides steering information plus other nav data such as times and wind velocities. Cross referencing the system to the outside world makes life much simpler, and the kit is updated at the turning points in order to keep it as accurate as possible. On time, and looking for the next turning point, a windmill on the edge of a wooded ridge. TANS gives four miles to go, and so it should show any time . . . Wooded ridge in the 2 o'clock! Follow it along to the left and . . . yes . . . a windmill – minus its sails. A 90-degree turn on to the next track, so roll on the bank, keep the yaw pedals central, play the lever against, the angle of bank and the Chinook flies around the corner just like a conventional aircraft – although in a much shorter distance. The reserve of power is excellent and the aircraft is responsive and agile – surprisingly so for its size and seemingly square, non-aerodynamic shape. Even a 30kt wind causes little trouble, although it is wise to anticipate sharp areas of turbulence caused by local wind effects on hills and valleys.

In between carrying out routine scan checks of aircraft systems and keeping an eye on troops or cargo, the crewmen act as the main element of

◄The CAD means that the Chinook must conceal the location of the LZ by sneaking in, offloading and sneaking out without being seen. With speed reduced, the aircraft can descend even lower and hide behind even the smallest feature.

▲Flying with an underslung load puts the aircraft higher and makes it more vulnerable: if you can see five miles then you can be seen from five miles.

'lookout'. Flying NOE means that the handling pilot must spend most of his time controlling the aircraft, whilst glancing around all the while to scan the horizon; the other front-ender shares time between navigating and 'lookout', but the latter is very restricted because of the aircraft's configuration. Each rear crew member has an area of responsibility to cover: the No 2 from the front door scans from as far forward as he can see back to the 6 o'clock and the No 1 crewman from that point to as far forward on the other side of the airframe as possible.

'Bogey, three o'clock, three miles. Left to right.'

'Tally! Number two padlock.'

There is every chance that the aircraft has not seen the helicopter and so to react too early would be counterproductive – it is better to watch and wait, trying to find even more cover. A sharp manoeuvre would almost certainly give the aircraft's position away by a glint of the rotor or a sudden perceived movement where a moment ago there was none. The commentary on where the aircraft is and what it is doing keeps the front end informed as the 'padlock' is passed from one crewman to the other until the aircraft vanishes from sight. There will be others, and the vigil cannot be relaxed for a moment.

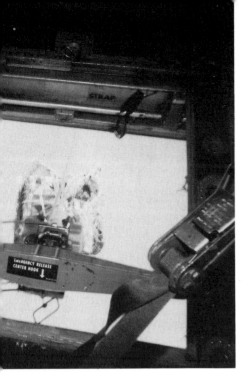

▲ A watchful eye as the aircraft keeps as low and fast as it can – if there are any problems, the underslung load can be released in a moment. (Paul Jackson)

◄ Defence suppression is provided by a machine gun mounted in the doorway (although this is not an option which the squadrons currently rehearse).

Air threats are not the only ones to worry about: for the ultra low-flying helicopter one of the biggest threats comes from birds. Birds and aircraft do not mix, and to hit a flock of even smallish birds can prove disastrous. A cry of 'Birds!' from the front end gives the rear crew an instant to brace for the sudden violent manoeuvre followed by an equally violent reverse to get the aircraft back down out of sight. For the troops it is yet one more moment of discomfort as their stomachs leap one way and then the other.

Eight miles to the LZ – and the IP for the CAD should appear around the corner of the next ridge. From this point, the aircraft sinks even lower, often down until it is almost touching the ground. As the height is reduced so must the speed be decreased, to allow for manoeuvre avoidance as the route down the 50,000-scale map is followed bit by bit. Down to 50ft and speed back to sneak along a line of trees and around an isolated farmhouse; drop down into an almost imperceptible fold in the ground between two fields. Suddenly . . .

'Break left . . .! SAM four o'clock coming towards! Flare gone!'

The tell-tale smoke trail of a shoulder-launched infra-red homing missile is picked up by the crewman and the pilot throws the aircraft into a violent manoeuvre whilst the crewman hits the flare button to fire off an IRD (infra-red decoy). The white-hot flare provides a much better target for the missile and the helicopter resumes its approach to the LZ. The CAD is even more important now as enemy troops are, without doubt, in the area! One route in and one route out . . . Four miles to go – time to get the back end ready for the LZ . . . Red light on and pre-landing checks complete. The plan is to carry out a run-on landing as the quickest way of getting into position. Two miles to go . . . Pass down the left of a ruined church so the tracking looks good, over a small rise in the ground, and the LZ should appear. Assess the final terrain, cover and

► Approaching the LZ at the edge of a wood . . . Keep below the tree-line, pick a spot, and set the aircraft up for the landing. (Paul Jackson)

wind to decide on the approach to give the best chance of getting into position first time – leaving room for the other Chinooks to get in with their loads.

An assessment of the landing area is made in seconds as the aircraft is positioned for its approach, and the MAOT presence means that no recce of the site is necessary. Without this knowledge that the site has been surveyed as suitable and dangerous areas highlighted, a quick visual recce of the LZ would have been needed – with the consequent delays in dropping off the troops and additional exposure to enemy attention. Speed is reduced as the aircraft descends towards the chosen spot . . . Assessment of the landing area itself – surface condition and type, slope, and so on. Commentary from the rear:

'Tail clear . . . Clear forward and down . . . Clear below, slight tail-wheel down-slope.'

Speed continuing to trickle back as the ground approaches . . . 20kt as the rear wheels touch . . . The aircraft rolls forward with the nose 10 degrees in the air. As the speed decays away to zero so the nose is lowered to the ground:

'LCTS to ground. Clear ramp down.'

At the same instant the ramp control lever is operated at the rear right-hand side of the Chinook and the hydraulic ramp swiftly lowers . . . Green light on, 'thumbs up' from the crewman, and the troops are on the way out of the aircraft . . .

'Ramp down. Troops out . . . Six to go . . . Last man out . . . Ramp coming up . . . Ramp clear of ground. Clear above and behind.'

After a mere 20 seconds the aircraft is rising from the grassy surface into the air, turning and moving away over the LZ towards the exit route of the CAD. One minute later, three of the four helicopters have delivered their loads and are already back down at below 50ft, leaving the area to return for the next wave of troops. The aircraft with the underslung load arrives at the LZ and is marshalled to the drop points – no point just dumping it and then having to get someone to move it around by hand! Over the point under the direction of the crewmen, with the traditional commentary calling the pilot to a steady hover before easing down to take the tension off the strop and have the load disconnected.

Within minutes of the arrival of the first Chinook, the LZ is deserted: there is no sign that anyone has been there, all troops and equipment safely under cover.

FUTURE DEVELOPMENTS

The requirement for tactical troop and equipment lift will, if anything, increase over the next few years as it not only adds to a commander's flexibility but also acts as a force multiplier by allowing units almost to be in two places at once. The Chinook is well established in the role, and although the other TS helicopter, the Puma, has a vital part to play in the scenario it cannot perform the same herculean feats as its larger colleague. There is, therefore, no reason why the Chinook should not continue to provide RAF heavy lift TS for many years to come. Its one weak area is that of self-defence in a ground and air environment which is becoming increasingly hostile thanks to a proliferation of anti-helicopter weapons systems — itself proof that the helicopter is seen as a potent battlefield asset.

The new helicopter on the horizon is the EH.101, which is being developed as a joint European project by Westland and Agusta to fill a variety of military and civil roles. In performance and load capability this aircraft can certainly be seen as a Puma replacement, but it falls far short of the current characteristics of the Chinook.

TRANSPORT/SUPPLY

URING A NUMBER of campaigns, senior air commanders have promised their ground colleagues that they can be supplied from the air and advised them to 'stick it out'. The results have been very mixed: some attempts have failed miserably, such as that to supply the German forces surrounded at Stalingrad in 1943; others have met with rather more success, as in the Berlin Airlift of 1948. All represent an extreme application of one facet of air power – the ability to move men and material from Point A to Point B quickly and thus influence a military (or political) situation.

Of all the roles implied in air power, this was among the last to be developed, for the simple reason that aircraft capable of transport and supply tasks were not available in the early years. During the interwar period, general-purpose aircraft, and especially those of the Army Co-operation squadrons, included supply dropping amongst their many tasks. This usually involved attaching stores to the bomb carriers and thus re-supplying troop columns or isolated outposts. In addition, the true transport squadrons were employed in a rather more strategic sense and became involved in such activities as the evacuation of the Kabul Residence. Once again, it was the Second World War which provided the impetus for the requirement and the development that led to the true tactical supply aircraft.

The Germans developed the Ju 52 as an all-purpose supply and transport aircraft, but the RAF had nothing really equivalent until the arrival of the American-built Dakota in the spring of 1943. This aircraft demonstrated the true

▼ *The classic tactical supply aircraft – a Douglas Dakota of No 267 Squadron, seen in 1944. Without doubt the contribution made by Dakotas in support of ground forces (including supply dropping) was decisive in many campaigns of the Second World War.*

flexibility and potential of tactical transport/supply with its ability to operate out of small, semi-prepared airstrips, its load-carrying capacity and its sturdy construction and reliability. Dakotas performed the full range of tasks from troop transport and para-dropping to freight-hauling and supply-dropping (and many more besides); in a number of campaigns their contribution was decisive, one such being the airborne supply of the Chindits in the jungles of Burma.

The Dakota retained these roles in the postwar period although it was gradually replaced by other types, none of which was able to perform quite the same range of tasks. Various 'bush-fire' campaigns since 1945 have continued to highlight the importance of the rapid movement of men and material, as evidenced by the RAF's continuing development of TS. The latest in the line of aircraft performing these tasks is also the one closest in capability to the classic Dakota – the Lockheed Hercules.

THE AIRCRAFT

Designed initially to meet a 1951 USAF Tactical Air Command specification for a tactical transport, the Hercules has for the last twenty years been the backbone of the RAF's tactical transport fleet. The type entered service with the RAF in 1967 as the Hercules C.1 (C-130K), XV176, the first aircraft, having made its first flight in October 1966. With its 92-troop or 20,259lb payload, the Hercules has shown itself to be a superb aircraft and one for which the oft-quoted 'flexibility' of air power has proved to be second nature. The payload is particularly significant when looking at the types of strips into and out of which the 'Herc' has been forced to operate – often no more than a small patch of, if you are lucky, semi-prepared dirt! The aircraft does not have to land to deliver its load but can drop its troops or supplies by a variety of techniques. It truly is a flexible workhorse.

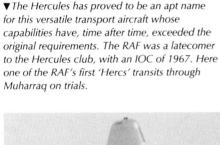

▼ *The Hercules has proved to be an apt name for this versatile transport aircraft whose capabilities have, time after time, exceeded the original requirements. The RAF was a latecomer to the Hercules club, with an IOC of 1967. Here one of the RAF's first 'Hercs' transits through Muharraq on trials.*

The basic airframe has been the recipient of numerous modifications, resulting in aircraft ranging from 'one-offs' such as the RAF's meteorological research Hercules to those undergoing a series of mods such as the USAF's gunship variants. In all that it has done, worldwide and for numerous air forces, the Hercules has achieved an outstanding reputation for reliability and sturdiness. In 1978 the decision was taken to enhance the carrying capability

◄'. . . Take this point as a TAP for the first run – it should be visible from about three miles at 250ft . . .'

◄Crew brief – running through the standard briefing format by pilot and nav. The time for questions is now and not as the load is about to be released.

◄At the aircraft, the front-end and back-end crews get together for the first time. The load is confirmed as checked, mission details are re-briefed and overall safety procedures are outlined.

▲ *One of the great advantages of the Hercules is its ability to operate from semi-prepared strips – although the luxury of a runway is always appreciated!*

of the RAF's Hercules fleet by adding a 15ft fuselage extension as fillets in front of and behind the wing, the new designation being C.3.

THE MISSION

The tasking signal confirms the details of the outline sortie received by the squadron a few days previously – a request for a Hercules to carry out supply-dropping in support of ground forces engaged in a search-and-destroy mission. The sortie is scheduled for 1 February, with a P-HR (drop time) for the aircraft of 1030. The aircraft is allocated its route timings and DZ (Drop Zone) coordinates as well as load details and any other information appropriate to the mission. The crew having been designated by the various sections of the squadron, initial planning is down to the navigator and co-pilot.

The first thing to do is to look at the DZ details and plan the final approach. This is the crucial part of the mission as the only reason for getting airborne is to drop the supplies in exactly the right place and at the right time – fail to do this and the whole mission has been a waste of time. A 1:50,000 scale map of the area gives an accurate planning format: DZ plotted, plus any restrictions, and the selection of an appropriate TAP (Target Acquisition Point) – the principle is the same as any low-level IP-to-target run where accuracy within feet is essential.

Choose a TAP (terminal attack parameter) that is easy to find and one that fits the requirements, draw in the track from TAP to target (referred to also as the IP, for impact point, in the world of TS) and study the line for obvious features that will make good navigational references on the run-in – an isolated farmhouse or the corner of a clump of trees, a minor road junction or a water tower. With the TAP-to-IP plan complete, the rest of the route can be worked out.

The mission time of two hours allows for a good, long, low-level phase before the drop itself and means that the sortie can go from Lyneham to North Wales and then down through the middle of Wales before turning towards Salisbury Plain and the DZ. Out with the half-million Low-Flying Chart and a ruler, pick up a brown felt-tip plan and make a start – who needs planning computers? The main planning aid is a '210-knot' piece of string. Although the basic route is constructed around a series of straight lines from point to point, these are only used for fixing reference into the nav kit – the doppler track and position. The actual route flown between each of the points will curve from side to side, deviating away from the mean by as much as 10 miles, with the purpose of making maximum use of any ground cover.

The Hercules low-level sortie is planned at 250ft and 210kt air speed, the latter allowing for variations in aircraft speed to make up or lose time and so keep to the overall mission time and achieve the TOT at the DZ. To allow for any major problems here, such as the aircraft not being available on time, the route includes a few points at which 'corners can be cut', thus saving time by flying fewer miles. Passing down through Wales also provides a good opportunity to fit in a few dummy DZ runs. TAP-to-IP runs are drawn up – a wood on a facing slope as a pre-TAP, leading the eyes into the TAP of a road bridge over a small river – down the run with features highlighted, looking for the IP of an isolated telephone box (not so easy now that these are no longer painted red!).

Stand back and take a look at the planning to see that it all makes sense – low-level maps with distance and timing marked on, TAP-to-IP maps for the dummy runs and live supply drop. Looks good. Both co-pilot and navigator have copies of the maps and the nav also has his flight plan with full details of the route, timings and fuel plan. Nothing more to do until the day of the mission.

It is 0630, and pilot, co-pilot and navigator gather at the Met Office to hear the latest scientific estimate on what the weather gods are up to. With a westerly airflow over the southern half of the country there should be few problems: scattered cloud with a base around 2,500ft (that will take out the tops of some of the hills in Wales) and visibility of the order of six miles. No changes required to the route other than to note that the aircraft might have to sneak down some of the Welsh valleys to avoid cloud. A final check of the route area in planning confirms that all is okay and that the mission can proceed. Meanwhile, out on the pan, the Engineer is giving the aircraft a good check-over. The Loadmaster has been at the aircraft for some time and in due course the load arrives ready for positioning on the aircraft. Some are easy, others are more akin to fitting a quart into a pint pot. With the Tactical Role Checks on conveyor, rollers, barriers and other equipment complete, the load itself is checked over by the 'Loadie' and the despatchers from 47 AD: load the right way round, parachutes in place and connected correctly, weight of load . . . all good for the planned AE (auto-extraction) of the containers. Moved into position on the ramp for a further set of checks and then pushed into its flight station within the aircraft. Final Check, to make sure that nothing will go wrong – a few tons of metal containers being dragged out of the back of the aircraft could cause an enormous amount of damage . . . such as taking the back end of the aircraft off! Every check is vital.

Ninety minutes to 'brakes off', and time for the first briefing. Pilot, co-pilot and navigator use a check-list style of briefing to ensure that all the essential items are covered – Time Check, task outline, intelligence, documentation, aircraft, timings, weather, departure, nav brief, drop details, communications, emergencies. Nothing left out, and all happy with how the mission will progress.

Out at the aircraft, and the first time that the entire crew is gathered together, comes the second briefing – essential details of the mission, plus the all-important safety and emergencies brief, much of the latter concerning actions required in the event of problems with the load during the drop. A quick check shows that the mission is about on time – just a couple of minutes late, and that can be made up during the start-up and taxi. Starting-up at base means that ground crew are available to assist, but one of the features of the Herc is its capability to operate on its own: the aircraft needs no external help to get the engines going and the crew can cover the routine procedures and fix any small snags which might occur. The standard practice is for the Loadie to stay outside the aircraft, 'connected' to the rest of the crew by intercom on his 'long lead', to supervise the start. Twenty minutes to brakes time as the No 3 engine turns over . . . Indications good – settled down and readings normal.

'Clear four.'

Four fingers are held up by the Loadie in confirmation: 'Four clear.'

'Starting four now . . .'. Hit the starter button whilst at the same time the Engineer opens the bleed air valve. The Allison turboprop is a reliable engine and a good starter, and within seconds the indications stabilize. The other two engines are quickly brought to life and the throb of the four turboprops reverberates through the airframe. All indications are good – ten minutes to go and time to taxi out. Unfortunately, the aircraft is crammed into a small parking space and there is no way of getting out by going forwards, so engage the engines into reverse thrust to move the aircraft backwards, with the Loadmaster acting as guide and mentor! A neat trick, but a very valuable one when space is tight.

'Clear behind, straight back . . . Ten, five, two, one . . . Start turn now. With the back down and leaning around watching the area behind the aircraft, the Loadmaster acts as the 'eyes' of the backwards-moving Hercules.

'Turning to port now.'

'Turn looks good – keep it coming.'

Clear of the obstacles and happy that the aircraft can taxi normally, the Captain cancels the reverse thrust and calls for the rear doors to be closed.

With its noticeable tendency to 'waddle', the Hercules moves along the taxiway to the holding point. Final checks on systems en route . . . Pre Take-off Checks . . . Clearance to go . . . Line up on the centreline without stopping, a rolling take-off. Throttles forward, keep the aircraft straight using the nosewheel steering until the airflow over the control surfaces is sufficient for rudder authority. After a slow start, the speed rapidly builds up . . . 'Rotate' – stick back and the Hercules lifts into the air . . . 'Gear and flaps,' and the aircraft is climbing away and turning on to the first heading.

▼ Backed out of its parking slot using reverse thrust, the Herc is now clear to taxi to the runway. (Paul Jackson)

◄ Map-reading and navigating from the right-hand seat. With the general direction confirmed, the Herc is free to manoeuvre to make best use of ground features.

Ten minutes later the Herc has settled down into the first leg of the low-level route. In the right-hand seat, the co-pilot glances from map to outside world and back again, checking the position of the aircraft against the planned line over the ground. While the visibility is good, the idea is to pick up a feature a few miles away as a reference and get the pilot to put the aircraft in the correct relationship to that feature.

'See that isolated wood in the eleven o'clock, Captain?'

'Put me half a mile to the right, clear to manoeuvre.'

The nav, likewise, is scanning the ground and relating actual features to planned position; with a 'long lead' plugged in, he can stand behind the co-pilot for the best view of the outside but also move back to his console to update the nav kit if required. Although accurate route nav is achieved via the 'Mark I eyeball' and the age-old left and right corrections, it is essential to keep the nav kit up to date – *all* nav systems degrade with time, and the Herc's is amongst the oldest systems in use at low-level. The kit will come into its own if the aircraft has to re-route, perhaps for weather or for a major change in timing – hence the need to keep it accurate.

'Nav, in one minute an update at thirteen to go and half a mile left.' . . . 'Nav, thirteen to go, half left, ready ready now.' On the 'Now', the nav updates the doppler kit with the visual fix.

'Albert' is not a combat machine in respect of mixing it with fighters, and so it is essential for all members of the crew to scan the horizon for other aircraft. This is one of the major factors in the style of low flying practised by the TS crews: go and hide from everybody – find all the small creases and folds in the landscape, squeeze down into a shallow valley or round the side of a hill, and keep all the turns gentle. This is why the straight doppler tracks are not flown – unless there is no other way. Nevertheless, 'lookout' is vital: if you see the threat early enough you have a chance of ducking down behind a hill, changing course and, hopefully, avoiding trouble. If it's a late spot, then at the very least the aircraft can be put into its best fighting stance – eyes covering every side to prevent the sneak attack and aircraft configured for manoeuvring. Most fighter pilots who have had to tackle a Herc at low level will testify how difficult it is to get in for a shot! You certainly can't outrun the fighter, but you can probably out-turn it.

Airborne for 60 minutes, and the Loadie starts another set of 'scan checks' down the back end, inside the aircraft, on equipment and looking for leaks, and outside to check the wings and engines. With the movement of the aircraft, the

►▲▼ Cleaned up and ready to drop down to low-level. At high power settings the engines become rather smoky – a characteristic of the Herc and one which could give away the aircraft's position and of which the crew must remain aware.

◀ '. . . Put me over the right-hand side of the dam . . .'

chains holding the load might have slackened a little, so a judicious bit of tightening keeps everything safely in place. Over the right-hand edge of the dam, check the computer position again with an overhead fix: on track but the timing has slipped by 30 seconds, so push the speed up to 220kt to trickle it back by the next turning point.

'P minus twenty.'

'Loadie – Captain. Prepare for action, prepare the load.'

Twenty minutes to the drop time for the DZ. From now on, attention is focused on the main point of the mission – to drop the load on time on the IP. Through the pre-drop checks, despatchers remove the securing chains from the load, leaving just the safety chain.

'P minus two minutes.'

'Two minutes. Action stations!'

The last minutes before the drop run are occupied with a myriad checks, all of which have the sole purpose of ensuring that everything goes smoothly. With the safety chain removed, the load needs only gravity to set it moving. Speed comes back, ready for opening the doors.

The TAP should show from about five miles, which will give plenty of time to get a good 'on top' fix and line up on the inbound track. Check in with the DZ ground party. The DZ party confirm that all is set and that the marker panels are laid out in accordance with the standard pattern for the expected load. The UHF link with the DZ party is an important element in getting the supplies in the right place. In a tactical environment the party would also provide essential information on DZ restrictions, threat areas or any changes of plan.

'On top . . . Now!' A fix into the nav kit, and doppler to 'Expanded' to increase the accuracy of its calculations. Ramp and doors opened as the aircraft settles down into the 1:50,000 run. Into the description of the first check feature . . . Down the left-hand side of the village . . . over the isolated farmhouse . . . On track, and the timing looks good.

'Fifteen seconds.'

Using the '50,000' map, the aircraft can be kept within yards of its planned run-in track. The ideal is to be smack on track and on planned heading a little way before the DZ, to make sure that the entire load lands within the designated drop area. Five miles to go, and the dayglo panels of the DZ markings should show any time. The CARP (Calculated Air Release Point) checks out with the latest information, so, all being well, the load will drift on to the IP.

Three miles out, the navigator takes over the visual nav – navigation now is by reference to the area beyond the target and by monitoring the nav kit. The run so far has been good and the aircraft is nicely lined up for an accurate drop; any correction from now on needs to be small to keep within the parameters. Stay low as long as possible, but every type of load has a set minimum drop height and so at some stage the aircraft has to climb . . .

'Pop up, pop up, go!' Convert any excess speed into height to achieve the planned dropping parameters for speed and height. It's a three-dimensional problem with track and height, with the added requirement to hit a target speed within a couple of knots.

'Red on . . . Red on!'

'Green on . . . Green on!'

The instant the call is made, the co-pilot punches the release button to initiate the auto-release sequence. In reality it is an auto gravity extraction, as the 'prime mover' for the load is indeed gravity, causing it to slide earthwards over the rollers as the aircraft climbs gently. The movement of the load is discernible by the change in the aircraft's trim – plus the confirmation from the back end by the Loadie . . .

'Extractor released, barrier broken, load moving . . . Load gone!' All in the space of a few seconds, as the 'express train' of metal containers exit the rear of the aircraft.

The parachutes deploy to stabilize the load and drift it to the waiting troops below. By the time the load has travelled its few hundred feet to earth, the

▼ *In the dark recess of the fuselage, the despatchers prepare the load. Theirs is an uncomfortable world as the aircraft bounces around at low-level.*

▲◀A final turn to go over the TAP on the run-in heading . . . Speed back ready to lower the ramp. *(Paul Jackson)*

◀The load is pulled out of the aircraft and within seconds the main parachutes deploy to slow the descent and, if the CARP was correct, ease the load on to the DZ. *(Paul Jackson)*

▲The number of parachutes to a load depends on its type and, to a lesser extent, the type of release. *(Paul Jackson)*

▶On its special platform with shock-absorbent features, the vehicle suffers no damage and the experts free it from its cage within minutes. *(Paul Jackson)*

Hercules has closed up its doors, increased speed and left the area, descending back down to low-level away from any prying eyes. The DZ party confirms the accuracy of the drop, and air supply is alive and well.

FUTURE DEVELOPMENTS
The RAF Hercules fleet is now almost 25 years old and there is no doubt that it cannot continue its stressful job for ever. However, there are no firm (announced) plans for a replacement, although rumours of a replacement have been surfacing since the early 1980s! The latest plan, but one that is also now gathering dust, is for a completely new tactical transport, and a variety of possibilities have been put forward with a view to European collaboration. But the Hercules production line is still running, and more aircraft could be acquired if necessary – and as time passes this seems a more likely path to follow. The role of tactical transport/supply will remain a vital one, and so an aircraft must be found, or developed, to meet the continuing requirement.

◀▲▼Two hours and forty minutes since take-off – most of it spent at low-level weaving around valleys. A quick cup of coffee, and then into the debrief session for the flight deck crew – what was good, what was not so good.

| Nimrod |

ANTI-SUBMARINE WARFARE

I N THE LATTER half of 1942, German U-boats were sinking an average of 750,000 tons of Allied shipping a month, and the Battle of the Atlantic was being lost. Not only were the vital cargoes not getting through, but ships and merchant seamen were going down faster than they could be replaced. Within a year the situation had changed and the U-boat's 'happy time' was over as their losses rose dramatically. The turnabout was in large part due to the increase in the anti-submarine capability of Coastal Command: air cover over the convoys in previously unguarded areas meant decreased losses in shipping, and even if an aircraft did not achieve a kill on its U-boat at the very least it prevented an attack on the convoy, with every chance that the enemy would be unable to find it again.

The lesson had been a long time in the learning and the experiences of the First World War appeared to have been forgotten. In the interwar period a number of RAF flying-boat squadrons had an anti-submarine role, although often this simply involved patrols around the fleet to locate submarines and then direct surface vessels to the area. Developments in airborne anti-submarine tactics and weapons fell behind those of the enemy, partly because the Admiralty considered that the shipborne asdic system had made the submarine so vulnerable as to be redundant! The eventual realization that this was not so led to much improvisation and, ultimately, success.

The lesson was not forgotten again in the postwar period, and aircraft have remained a vital link in the defence chain against submarines. The helicopter has, of course, come into its own in the short-range point-defence ASW scenario for naval task force protection. Nevertheless, the long-range maritime patrol aircraft (LRMP) has a vital strategic role to play, with its ability to set up search-and-block patterns to prevent hostile submarines moving through critical defence zones, and since the development of the nuclear-missile-armed submarine, the airborne AS role has become even more vital. The ability of the

▶ Aircraft versus submarine, 1943: a U-boat is caught on the surface by an aircraft of No 233 Squadron. After a period of seeming invulnerability, the U-boats suddenly found themselves attacked from the air and losses began to mount.

submarine to sink major surface vessels was demonstrated in the Falklands War of 1982 with the loss of the Argentinian cruiser *General Belgrano*, and the threat to the Task Force from Argentinian submarines caused many a sleepless night – especially because there was no land-based maritime air cover.

THE AIRCRAFT

Intended as a replacement for the Shackleton, the Nimrod was developed from the successful Comet airliner. It was designed to combine the advantages of high-altitude performance and fast transit speeds, with low wing loading and good low-speed manoeuvring capabilities in order to operate in its primary roles of ASW, surveillance and anti-shipping strike. The first two aircraft were conversions from Comets, whilst the first production Nimrod MR.1 flew in June 1968, the type entering service the following year. It was the first land-based four-jet maritime recce aircraft to enter service, and as such was a world leader. In due course Nimrods equipped five RAF maritime squadrons, and the four UK-based units still operate the type today. Two major upgrades have taken place – to MR.2 standard in the mid-1970s, and to MR.2P standard (AAR-capable) in 1982 as a direct consequence of the Falklands conflict. In recent years attempts have been made to keep the aircraft up to date by fitting new avionics, ESM (electronic support measures) equipment and weapons systems – a sensible and effective policy as there is nothing wrong with the basic airframe or its capabilities. Nimrod, 'The Mighty Hunter' is certain to remain operational for a number of years.

It must be borne in mind that ASW is but one of the many roles which the Nimrod performs: it is also a potent anti-shipping aircraft, and it is a vital link in the SAR organization.

THE MISSION

'Task in, crew to Ops'. The arrival of another tasking signal from Northwood, and crew and aircraft are allocated for a 'search, locate and destroy' anti-submarine patrol. The previous scene, with the air crew sitting around drinking coffee, waiting for the call from Ops, is transformed into an organized bustle as crew planning commences. Each member of the crew has a specific task to perform as part of the overall planning sequence – and there is not much time before the first briefing! The Mission Support System provides the crucial information to generate the MCB (Maritime Crew Brief), with the basic details of the task worked out and coordinated and then passed on to the crew for detailed planning. With this to hand, the crew can begin to read themselves in to the mission requirements.

Co-pilot and 'Routine Nav' work together on the route and general area details, including the latest data from the intelligence people on activity and possible threats in the operational area. From this point, the Routine Nav becomes, in effect, the 'sortie secretary', recording and analyzing inputs from the other members of the crew; this task becomes even more important in the air when the details he has recorded can be used, at any time, to 'revise' the mission's progress.

The TacNav (Tactical Navigator) concentrates on the operational area, planning the mission tactics – based on the intelligence so far received but in the full knowledge that his basic plan will almost certainly have to change as the mission progresses. Although the First Pilot oversees the entire mission plan, it is to the area of tactics, with the TacNav, that he devotes most of his attention;

◄ The world's first four-jet maritime patrol aircraft, Nimrod entered service in 1969 and proved to be an immediate success. In essence the aircraft is little more than a platform for the array of sensors and weapons which it carries.

in the operational area these two will work very closely together, coordinating the inputs of the entire crew. The seven Sensor Operators carry out various tasks – from mission planning by the Lead Dry, looking at the EW aspects, and Lead Wet, the all-important acoustic conditions in the target area, to arranging safety equipment and organizing rations for the sortie. The final member of the crew, the Engineer, has, meanwhile, been checking on the aircraft details and, in liaison with the TacNav's requirements, making sure that the right quantity of the right sonobuoys are loaded.

Thirty minutes to briefing, and the mission details are nearing completion – operational area plotted, combined search pattern tactics outlined, route details complete, intelligence data analyzed and plotted, aircraft load confirmed. A final check around the crew for any other inputs . . . a last-minute change in intelligence puts a Soviet 'Krivak' guided missile frigate in the area – its SAN-4 missiles are a formidable short/medium range defensive system and it is a vessel to keep well clear of if at all possible. This general briefing by the MSS staff takes about fifteen minutes. Data are stored on computer and flashed up on to the screens in the briefing room. The overall intelligence plot reveals the complexity of the situation and highlights the need for ESM monitoring during the transit to the task area.

Load all the kit on to the crew bus and move out to the aircraft, 1 hour 20 minutes to take-off . . . The hydraulics snag which the Engineer discovered on his earlier inspection of the aircraft has been rectified, and the Nimrod looks all set to go – if all the systems check out. Each member of the crew must carefully check his area of responsibility and systems: nav kit 'on', set and checked; computer programmed with the mission tape and route checked; TacNav's planned mission load of sonobuoys checked by the 'wet men' and programmed into the computer. The nav confirms that the weapons load is as programmed. The Stingray torpedoes in the bomb bay give the Nimrod a mighty punch. A more accurate description of this weapon would be an underwater guided missile, as Stingray works more like an AAM than a traditional torpedo. An acoustic homing system in the nose activates as the 'missile' enters the water and from that point the onboard computers take over and control the attack. The torpedo becomes a sub-hunter, the sensors and computers working out the ideal attack for the type of target detected. The net result is the best impact parameters for the highly effective shaped-charge warhead.

▶ *Every element of the complex systems which make up the Nimrod's operational capability must be checked and checked again. At each crew station, especially those of the Tactical Crew in the heart of the aircraft, every item is put through its paces and brought on line.*

▼◀▶ *A planning conference, and a few last-minute changes before the briefing. The major elements of the mission planning fall to the TacNav and co-pilot, although each member of the crew has a part to play.*

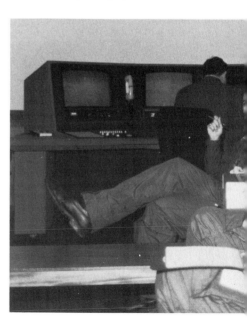

. . . Radios, radar, EW equipment – all are checked, and all form part of the Nimrod as a fighting system. The back of the aircraft is a hive of activity as each crew member runs through his pre-flights, cross-checking with other crew stations as required. The integration of all the individual elements is the key to the effectiveness of the system in its task of finding and killing submarines. A snag on the VDUs of the nav station needs the attention of a ground technician. How much delay will this cause? Can it be fixed? If not, can the mission go ahead without this item? A multitude of thoughts as the minutes tick away towards the brakes-off time. Try again to recycle the VDUs by switching on and off and resetting the circuit breakers . . . No joy, so one more go . . . The screens blink and then stabilize – as so often happens with electronic equipment, there doesn't appear to be anything wrong, and if at first it does not work, try it again!

At the front end it is the same for the pilots, with the aircraft and flight systems getting the 'once over'. Thirty minutes to take-off, so time to start the engines, and the crew check in to give status of systems, ready for the engine start . . . So far the systems look good. The Crew Chief confirms 'clear' for No 3 engine . . . Light up, the indications are good, and the gentle rumble through the airframe sounds and feels about right. The other three Rolls-Royce Spey 250s light up in turn and stabilize at idling as the Engineer surveys his panels for the least sign of any problem. These panels are, in effect, the 'health monitoring' of the aircraft's engines and associated systems, and the experienced Engineer will detect the slightest flicker of a needle, the merest hint of a flaw developing, long before the aircraft alarm systems will show it up.

At the end of the runway, with engines at full throttle, the aircraft judders under the strain, held by the brakes. Final checks, cleared to go . . . Brakes off,

and accelerate down the tarmac. Speed builds rapidly . . . 'VR' . . . Back on the stick, and the Nimrod rises into the air. Minutes later the aircraft is out over the sea and on its own. Although the task area is some way away there is no shortage of tasks to be performed, all with the aim of getting this potent weapon system to its designated area in one piece, on time and ready for action.

'Tactical checks outbound.'

The list is quickly completed to bring the aircraft systems on line, with weapons checked as serviceable but not yet armed. Much of the routine interchange of information between the Tac crew is made off the aircraft's intercom – a piece of data is passed from one computer screen to another, a shouted instruction or series of numbers is made – since to clutter up the 'airwaves' within the aircraft would be counterproductive. So much has to be relayed that there would hardly be a second of quiet! Keep the intercom for essentials!

ESM reports picking up a Soviet early warning radar, classified as probably a 'Headnet'. There are no other supporting electronic data, but a radar sweep confirms a surface contact in the area, assessed as 'likely to be a warship'. 'Headnet' is carried by numerous Soviet vessels. Some would pose an immediate threat, others not, but there is no point in taking the aircraft that way: an alteration of course keeps the aircraft well away from any trouble.

Listen and look: monitoring the systems from radar to EW helps build up the picture of what is really happening in the area rather than the theoretical scenario provided at the planning stage. Does it change the overall tactical plan? What is the significance of that piece of EW information? ESM reports an airborne pick-up, classified as a 'Bear-D' – recorded by Routine Nav, relayed to Maritime HQ . . . The picture is continually changing, and the TacNav's screen takes on the role of tactical map of his area of interest. Approaching the task area now, and time to go down to low-level.

'Tactical checks on task.'

This brings the aircraft into a state where it is ready for action. The weapons are checked and armed and the sonobuoy launchers loaded. Now comes the final tactical briefing by TacNav for radar search and a carefully structured pattern (field) of sonobuoys. Level off, a radar check to assess the picture: 'On' . . . a quick check on clarity and the discrimination of the picture . . . 'Off'. The idea is to try and achieve surprise, to catch the submarine unawares so that it cannot dive into the sanctuary of the depths. The general

▲ One of the assets of the jet-powered Nimrod is its overall performance, including high transit speeds which enable it to get to the task area quickly. Like many other aircraft, Nimrod has acquired external 'lumps and bumps' to improve its capability – the AAR probe at the front, the MAD tail at the back, the wing-tip LORAL ECM pods and, on occasion, underwing Sidewinder missiles. (Paul Jackson)

▶ The front end of the aircraft has restricted visibility – all that was needed for the era in which the Comet airliner, from which the Nimrod arose, was developed. Two pilots and the Flight Engineer monitor and manage the systems of the aircraft itself rather than the operational suite.

surface plot of the area, if any, has already been established on the screen by the radar search from outside the area, and the combined search pattern can be established. As the aircraft flies its pre-planned radar search the pattern of sonobuoys is dropped until the 'field' is complete.

With the search pattern established, the routine of looking and listening becomes even more intense. Those members of the crew not actively engaged with monitoring systems scan the waters and sky from the bulging domes of the port and starboard beam positions for contacts and threats – low-level over the sea is no place to get bounced by an aircraft (even though Nimrods have been seen sporting a pair of Sidewinder missiles for self-defence)!

Acoustic reports a contact from a sonobuoy suggesting that a diesel submarine is in the area recharging its batteries, the diesel engine noise being picked up by the sonobuoy:

'Captain, Acoustics . . . Contact on Lofar . . . Analyzing.'

Almost instantaneously the situation is assessed and the aircraft turned

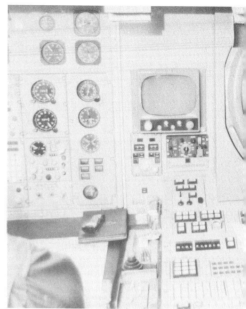

▲◄ Transiting to the task area at medium-level, the Nimrod is very vulnerable and must rely on its passive sensors, such as the wing-tip pods, to collect and analyze electronic data to reveal potential threats. If you know it's there, then you can avoid it. (Paul Jackson)

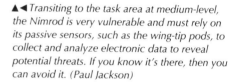

▲ The nav station, with the Routine Nav to the left and the Tactical Nav to the right. Amongst the array of buttons and screens, the most important is the large circular tactical display screen – in essence the battle management system.

◄ Low-level over the sea is where the aircraft is at home in its task of hunting and killing submarines.

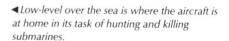

towards the relevant sonobuoy. The contact must be within an area centred on the sonobuoy, and it is from there that any attack should commence.

'Possible sub. Diesel sub.'

Rolled out heading towards the area, acoustics listening out for sonobuoy data and relaying to the TacNav, and the battle plan formulates. Get to the target before it detects the aircraft and tries to escape, and set up for a good first-pass attack – while preparing a pattern for any target-area search should the submarine vanish at the last minute. Relay data to the radar ops screen for the radar search area and pattern required when called for, plus a quick verbal brief on how the TacNav wants to play it . . . Call for radar 'On' at the appropriate range to scan the contact area . . .

'Captain, Radar: high-confidence snort two-seven-zero degrees, fifteen miles.'

With this data fed into the CTS (Computer Tracking System), the nav initiates a steer towards the target. Twelve miles to contact area, all systems look good, still held on acoustics and radar. The weapons are primed and ready, the aircraft running in at maximum speed to reduce the sub's evasion time . . . The pilots begin to scan the area ahead of the aircraft – surely the sub must dive before the aircraft reaches it? Very few people are lucky enough to get in a full visual attack.

'On top . . . Now, now, now.'

Overhead the in-contact sonobuoy, and the attack continues.

'Captain, Radar. Contact lost. Sinker. Eleven miles.'

It is no great surprise that the aircraft has been detected and the sub has gone into an evasive dive. The tactical plan has allowed for this. Continue towards the datum to set up an attack pattern.

'Ten miles.'

'Action stations! Action Stations! Prepare for MAD!'

Acknowledgement of the MAD instruction confirms that yet another of the detection systems is ready to go. The Magnetic Anomaly Detector will detect any changes in the water caused by the passage of a large metallic object – like a submarine! TacNav briefs his final intentions for the attack.

'Four miles. Bomb doors. HRD.'

The underneath of the aircraft parts to reveal the weapons bay and its cargo of torpedoes.

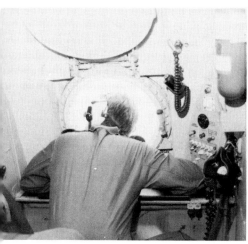

▲ One of the essential elements for attack and defence is to be able to look all around the aircraft. The port (as here) and starboard beam positions with their outward bulging windows give an excellent view to each side, and even towards the rear.

▶ An essential element of the combined search technique is the variety of sonobuoys which can be dropped to form a detection field. The sonobuoy launcher is prepared for action as the aircraft enters the task area. (Paul Jackson)

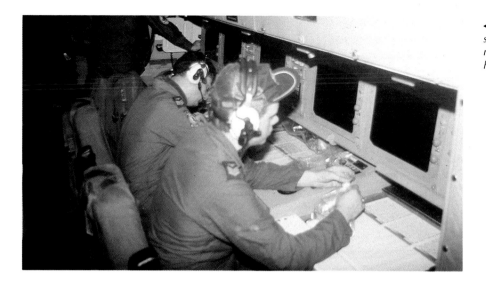

'One and a half miles. Searchlight.' As the co-pilot switches on the searchlight the nav calls that the aircraft has entered the likely MAD area and the pilot confirms that the aircraft is configured for MAD. Still no contact re-established, and it seems inevitable that a new pattern of sonobuoys will have to be laid. Overhead the datum, so lay a pattern of active sonobuoys around the target position. With the field set, the nav puts the aircraft into a MAD-trap circle around the area, waiting for any tell-tale indications, ready to let loose the torpedo.

And so the waiting game, cat-and-mouse, begins. The submarine will be looking for a way out of the trap – a change of speed, direction or depth – and the aircraft, with its array of sensors, will be looking and listening, predicting what its prey will try to do next. Some buoys are keyed to look for the sub that tries to run for it, others concentrate on the 'hider' who sits still and pretends not to be there.

'Captain, Acoustics. Active fix. One-eight-zero degrees.'

▶ '. . . One and a half miles. Searchlight on . . .'
The procedures are the same for a day or a
night attack, and so at the relevant distance the
powerful searchlight in the starboard wing is
activated.

The call from the acoustics monitor tells the TacNav where the contact is
with reference to a particular sonobuoy, and this is quickly assessed on the
tactical display. The display in front of the TacNav automatically takes on the
new data and shows the plot of the target position as a row of diamonds on the
screen. In theory, at any given time, the submarine is at the position of the last
diamond to be displayed. Select target tracker to bring the computer predictions
into the loop . . . A few more acoustic plots, and the computer gradually pins
the position of the target down . . .

With the call from the TacNav, the Nimrod swings round towards the in-
contact sonobuoy as the attack is set up. Prediction looks good, attack track
established, weapons selected and parameters set. Again the sonobuoy loses

▼ Bomb doors open, and the aircraft makes its
final adjustments prior to releasing the torpedo.

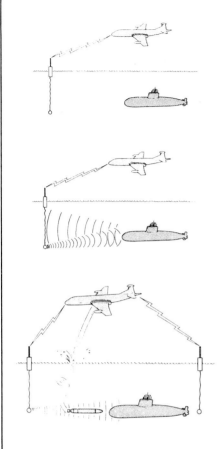

On arrival in the patrol area the first thing the crew do is lay out a pattern of sonobuoys. The sonobuoy can be likened to an electronic 'bug' – it enables the AEOp on board the aircraft to hear everything that is going on beneath the surface of the sea. After it strikes the water, the sonobuoy floats back to the surface and a radio aerial springs into place. Then a hydrophone (an underwater microphone) is released from the bottom of the cylinder and dangles from the end of a long cable, and the AEOp monitors the noises picked up by the hydrophone.

It is not an easy task, for there are many distracting sounds, some of which will be very much louder than the quiet enemy submarine which is seeking to avoid detection – merchant ships passing through the area, friendly warships with which the aircraft is cooperating, and the rumbles, groans and hisses from the sea itself and the creatures living in it all serve to hide the real quarry. The Nimrod crew must learn to ignore these distractions and go about their task with stealth so as not to reveal their presence.

On board the Nimrod the sound patterns passed back from the sonobuoys are displayed visually on a TV-like screen. By careful examination of various aspects of the pattern, the trained AEOp can distinguish the sounds he is looking for from those he is not. The operators can and do listen to the sounds, but most of the analysis is done on the visual display screens linked to some of the aircraft's very powerful computers.

Unless the Nimrod crew are lucky, it might be several hours before their quarry enters the 'bugged' area, in which case they will hear only the background noises, but once the faint noise of a submarine is detected the second phase of the hunt begins. At this stage the hunters know only that their quarry is present in one part of the 'bugged' area, but not exactly where. Their aircraft carries more complex types of sonobuoy which, still without revealing that a hunt is in progress, can pass back to the Nimrod the precise bearing from which the noises are coming. Two such buoys, dropped some distance on either side of the sonobuoy which had originally heard the submarine, can provide a pair of bearings which cross to show the exact location of the vessel; alternatively, the Nimrod can put down an active buoy, which transmits sonar 'pings' whose echoes betray the submarine's position. However, the submarines will then know that the hunters are closing in and they may try to make a dash for it. The Nimrod crew can then release a special torpedo which homes on to the submarine and removes it from the battle.

▼ As the Stingray clears the bomb bay its parachute drogue deploys to clear it from the aircraft's slipstream and ensure that it enters the water at the correct angle. (Marconi Underwater Systems)

▼▼ Water entry, and the highly sophisticated torpedo will enter its search, track and destroy routine. (Marconi Underwater Systems)

contact: the submarine has manoeuvred out of its area . . . Does the computer prediction cover the change? What is the submarine doing? There is no time to reestablish a sensor contact – continue on this attack or adjust the profile by trying to 'second-guess' the opposition . . .

'Hard right . . . Wings level.'

With the decision to take a manual correction, there is only time now for the nav to select the computer ballistics and finalize the attack. Countdown from 10 to zero . . . Hit the weapon release button and check that the orange light on the store select panel goes out. At almost the same instant the MAD mark corroborates the computer's calculations. The confirming call of 'Weapon away' comes from the crewman monitoring the bomb bay periscope as the Stingray torpedo clears the aircraft, its parachute deploys and it slices into the water.

Water entry is picked up by the acoustic monitors, who also confirm from the distinctive 'pinging' that the weapon is under way:

'Torpedo running.'

The aircraft is cranked into a holding pattern over the entry area, ready to make further attacks . . . The seemingly interminable wait whilst the torpedo runs its course – a matter of minutes at most, but feeling like much more.

'Loud underwater explosion.'

Confirmation that the lethal Stingray has found its target! A hit is a kill, as the chances of a diesel submarine surviving a Stingray impact are minimal. One down – but how many more might be lurking in the task area? There is no time to sit around. While the crew run through the post-incident check list, getting the aircraft systems set back to search mode, re-filling the sonobuoy launchers and selecting the next weapon, the Nimrod climbs back to patrol height and reestablishes the search pattern. These could be many more hours of looking and listening, and perhaps even another attack to carry out, before the patrol comes to an end and the aircraft recovers to base. The duration is limited more by the number of sonobuoys and weapons carried rather than by any other factor, since the Nimrod is AAR-capable and can call for a tanker if required. Airborne for four hours and time to replenish some of the energy expended on the first attack as the onboard galley comes into its own as a source of hot food!

FUTURE DEVELOPMENTS

The Nimrod has proved itself to be an outstanding aircraft for its designated roles, and as long as the aircraft's systems continue to be upgraded, to meet the changing requirements of its roles, then there is no reason why the aircraft should not keep going for many years. The next major update on the aircraft's systems is due to take place in the early 1990s, although details of what this will involve are not yet known. Perhaps the biggest 'gap' in the aircraft's capability is the lack of a computer data-link.

There is at present no firm plan for a Nimrod replacement, and if such did materialize it would almost certainly involve the purchase of one of the American LRMP aircraft now under consideration or development. The most likely candidate for this choice is the P-7, although certain aspects of this programme, including cost against performance, do not appear to be entirely satisfactory in RAF eyes.

THE PUBLIC FACE OF THE ROYAL AIR FORCE

THERE ARE TWO main ways in which the public observes a military aircraft – as a glimpse and a deafening roar as it passes overhead or, more conventionally, by visiting one of the many public air displays held during the summer. Military air displays have their origins in the 1920s with the great Hendon Air Pageants at which the RAF showed off its latest aircraft types and performed a series of 'set piece' events, from formation flying by the CFS and designated squadrons to the great 'air battles' where the attacking bombers were engaged and 'destroyed' by the nimble fighters.

The Second World War brought an end to formal displays such as these on any large scale. However, the achievements of RAF fighter pilots in the Battle of Britain became the focus for a new era of commemorative displays in the postwar period with the growth of the RAF Battle of Britain 'At Home' day. This type of display had two main purposes: first, to show the British public the current equipment and capabilities of its air force (and perhaps do some recruiting); and second, to raise funds for the RAF charities, primarily the RAF Benevolent Fund. These aims have remained essentially the same to the present day.

Before long, however, some of the atmosphere of the old Hendon Days began to reappear, with special set-piece actions and the growth once more of squadron display teams. By the mid-1950s, the scene had been set for the typical air display: the squadrons of the home station would appear in a variety of guises, including a formation team which would try to keep coming up with innovative ideas each year; one of the squadron aircraft would then do a solo stint, throwing the aircraft about; the latest RAF bomber and fighter would each take its turn in the aerial arena and show off its capabilities; and then the show would close with a display either by the 'home team' or by one of the speciality guests. This formula proved successful and in essence is still the one used today. At the same time there was the need to occupy the public with ground events, and so a wide range of aircraft types was scattered around the airfield as a static display with the crews standing by them to answer questions 'from the air-minded youth'.

Thus the style of RAF air displays gradually evolved, but as the RAF contracted so did the number of displays, until not every station put on an annual show. However, those which did put on displays could call on a wider range of participants and thus became showpieces for the RAF as a whole rather than local affairs. In general terms, one of each aircraft type within the UK is permitted to work up for a display season, although this responsibility is often rotated among the units. Other aircraft are permitted to make fly-throughs or low passes which do not involve sequenced manoeuvres – a way of bringing into the show aircraft which would otherwise not be seen. Variations occur during anniversary years, when a particular unit or aircraft type might take part in a limited number of displays; an example occurred in 1989, the 40th anniversary year of the Canberra, and various of these aircraft appeared and displayed at a number of shows. The other side of the coin is, of course, the

▲ No 39 Squadron DH 9As rehearse for one of the Hendon Pageant displays – the highlight of the prewar aviation year and a chance for the RAF to show itself to the public.

▶ Each year many thousands of people attend air displays throughout the UK. One of the largest is at RAF Finningley – a venue which attracts some 130,000 each year!

▶ As well as the 'routine' air shows, the RAF mounts special displays. For example, the celebrations at RAF Wyton in May 1989 to mark the 40th anniversary of the Canberra were restricted to ex-Canberra air crews, but with Press coverage the 'blue' Canberra, used to recreate the first flight of the type, was widely seen.

professional display team (as opposed to the squadron crew whose display career is decidedly part-time), and the RAF has perhaps the best known of all – the Red Arrows, of which more later.

There would be little point, in this chapter, in running through all the RAF types which currently appear on the air show circuit, so it is proposed merely to highlight the basic principles behind display flying by looking at a few typical examples, and adding a few words about the Red Arrows. No mention will be made of the vintage aircraft operated by the RAF, and likewise there is no space to deal with the dozens of aircraft which appear in the static displays – although in many ways these are better ambassadors to the public than their flying brethren as they can be seen at close range.

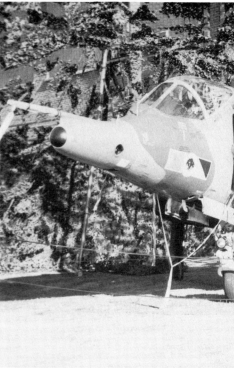

Flying a display routine is not a natural occupation for either the aircraft or the crew, except in the case of the specialist display team. The RAF organizes a great many air displays during a year, but the four largest are the official Battle of Britain displays at RAF Finningley, RAF Leuchars, RAF St Athan and RAF Abingdon. For the organizers of these shows the policy remains that of public relations and, as a secondary consideration, charity fund-raising. The aim of the display coordinator is to put on a balanced show which highlights the Royal Air Force, and to this end most shows concentrate on displays by current front-line aircraft plus the specialist teams (although recent years have seen increasing participation by the growing fleet of 'warbirds', to 'balance' the noise and speed of the fast jets and to add a historical perspective to the display). Another important aspect of such displays is NATO participation – it is important to emphasize the fact that the RAF is an integrated part of the NATO air component in the operational sense. The latter has suffered somewhat since 1989, with the *Luftwaffe* not participating in air displays following the Ramstein disaster and

▲◄► *An important element of any display is the array of static aircraft, i.e., those present which are not destined to be part of the flying display. Here the public can get up close to the aircraft and talk to the crews. Displays of weapons fits or operational scenarios, such as the Harrier 'hide', help to show the aircraft to the full.*

◄ *Reheat blazing, the GR.1 gets airborne to start its display.*

the almost yearly reduction in USAF participation because of 'funding difficulties'.

A Tornado GR.1 spends most of its operational life flying around at 420kt and 250ft, trying to keep out of trouble (i.e., not getting 'bounced' by anybody), attacking its simulated target (usually in company with up to seven other aircraft) and going home again; furthermore, it is quite happy to do this at night or in cloud. It does not fly tight manoeuvres around an airfield, do loops or barrel rolls or perform any similar aerial gyration. If the Tornado on the air display programme did a 420kt flypast at 250ft and then vanished into the distance the crowd would not be particularly impressed! The squadron chosen to provide the Tornado GR.1 display for a particular season of shows, therefore, must work up a crew and a display routine. The essence of any routine is to show the aircraft off to its best advantage, which means having a detailed knowledge of what it can and cannot do – a Tornado which tried to better an F-16's 360-degree turn would look foolish; it is more sensible, instead, to show the Tornado's own unique abilities and facets. Having been selected, the crew must then decide on the style of display and plan each individual movement with precision, to construct what amounts to an aerial ballet with the aircraft always in sight of the crowd and yet keeping the latter guessing as to what the aircraft will do next – and then, hopefully, surprising them with what it actually does.

Many hours are spent with the aircrew manual (the 'bible' of aircraft capability), pencil and paper as various combinations are examined as theoretical possibilities. Previous display routines, by Tornados and other

▶▲▼One of the unusual aspects of the Tornado is its 'swing-wing', and full use of this is made during the display to show the aircraft off in both high- and low-speed manoeuvres.

◄ *After only a few thousand feet of runway, the Tornado F.3 climbs away, tucking up its undercarriage.*

◄ *A rare sight at displays – a pair of Tornado F.3s with a Victor tanker, hoses deployed, simulating an air-to-air refuelling session. Both fighters carry a missile load.*

◄ *The mock refuelling and air combat over, the F.3s return to show off another of their capabilities – a very short field landing using the lift dump devices on the wings and the engine thrust reversers.*

aircraft, are analyzed for good ideas, and gradually a plan of action comes together. The usual time slot for a fast-jet routine at a display is of the order of 8–10 minutes, and every second must be accounted for. The paper routine is transferred to the air as aspects of the display are tested out and timed – something that looked good on paper often does not work at all in the air. Ideas come and go, manoeuvres are changed or adapted, and slowly the final ensemble fits together and begins to 'feel right' . . . a little bit more height on the second wing-over gives just the right timing to get the wings back for a high-speed pass into a tight turn, and so on.

The basic routine decided, the real test comes with the first full rehearsal – does the whole thing work, and what will it look like from the ground? The Tornado display for 1990 was flown by a TWCU crew and a No 27 Squadron crew, and the TWCU crew spent a great deal of time pondering on how best to display their aircraft whilst at the same time including a few items which have not been seen in previous Tornado shows. Rather than launch straight into the display from take-off, the aircraft 'arrived' from a holding point on a hidden approach, curving around in front of the crowd as if appearing from nowhere and then going into an initial series of manoeuvres in front of the onlookers. The main part of the display aimed at keeping the aircraft tightly in front of the crowd with a series of wing-overs, rolls and tight turns at various wing sweeps, with minor adjustments to make sure that the line for the next manoeuvre would work and keeping the vital checks going on position, height and speed. A small error in alignment could have made the entire manoeuvre look a complete shambles. Building up to the climax . . . Unload and run out slightly further so that speed could be built up on the final run-in for the high-speed pass into a vertical departure.

Every aircraft type has its own 'party piece'. The rest of the fast-jet types tend to do things similar to those demonstrated with the Tornado – and the 500kt arrival pass by the Buccaneer is without doubt a thing of beauty, often heightened by the vortices created by water vapour being squeezed out of the surrounding air. The large bulk of the Phantom pulling out of its loop and cranking over into a tight turn with the burners providing a deafening accompaniment is a sight, and sound, never to be forgotten. It is perhaps a sad fact that by the end of the 1990s the fast-jet RAF contribution to air displays will comprise only the Tornado in either its mud-moving or air defence guise – plus perhaps the Eurofighter if it has reached service by then.

The other operational types also fly their routines to show off the best facets

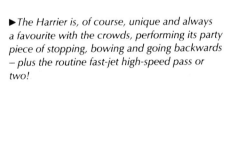

of the aircraft. The larger types have the advantage of size – big aircraft are instantly impressive even if they don't do very much! A 30-degree bank turn at 300ft with a Nimrod looks quite aggressive, especially if the bank is rolled on and off quickly. With airbrakes out and bomb doors open, the Nimrod goes into a left-hand break from its initial run-in . . . round the orbit using 60 degrees' angle of bank and setting up an attack configuration pass with the searchlight going on as the aircraft approaches the display line . . . turn back using a 90-degree bank and with the next pass as a landing configuration . . . clean up, full-power climbing turn (again using 90 degrees) and descending back along the crowd line . . . 300ft and 250kt, pull 2g and nose up to 50 degrees for a full power climb, rolling left to depart the display line. From start to finish a mere five minutes!

The Hercules has a series of spectacular events of its own, perhaps best described in the 'standard' commentary which accompanies the display:

Lyneham-based C-130 Hercules aircraft played a significant part in the Falklands conflict. The Hercules that you will see today will demonstrate its manoeuvrability and its ability to operate from short runways. It was that capability – to take off and land on short strips – that meant, apart from the Harrier with its vertical take-off and landing, that the Hercules was the only RAF aircraft that was able to operate from the 4,000ft badly damaged runway at Port Stanley. The strong, rugged construction of the aircraft, featuring extremely powerful brakes and reverse thrust, allows it to operate from dirt strips or fields. The Captain today comes from the Special Forces flight of No 47 Squadron and has over 7,000 hours on the Hercules.

After a tight, low-level circuit, the aircraft will make a tactical landing at reduced airspeed, just a few knots above stalling speed, and it will then stop as quickly as possible. As it stops, watch the rear of the aircraft and you will see the rear cargo door lower to the ground and Scorpion tanks emerge ready for action. It is planned that from touchdown to take-off should take less than 75 seconds. Once the tanks are clear, the rear doors close as the aircraft backs up to ensure that enough runway is available for a tactical take-off. Note the surprisingly short distance for take-off and the steep climb out – the aim is to climb away as steeply as possible from obstructions and small-arms fire.

As the aircraft turns back towards us it will be configured for a simulated stores drop. We can see that once again the rear doors are open, whilst the aircraft flies level at slow speed, simulating the low-level free drop of grain during the Ethiopian Famine Relief. The Captain demonstrates how manoeuvrable this 50-ton aircraft is by performing a series of high-speed turns before setting up for the famous 'Khe Sahn' approach. The aircraft will run in at altitude and then suddenly drop from the sky – a manoeuvre developed by the Americans during the Vietnam War in an attempt to avoid small-arms fire. The aircraft stays high until over the 'safe' area, then descends steeply on to the runway, stopping in a short distance to clear the runway.

Sitting up on its rear wheels as if begging, moving backwards at over 50kt and then taking to the air still flying backwards – this is but one of the many

◄ To see such a large aircraft as the Nimrod displayed with agility and speed comes as something of a surprise!

▶▲▼In the midst of 'battle', a Hercules touches down and lowers its ramp. Tanks race out and 'engage' the 'enemy' whilst attack aircraft scream overhead in support.

'party pieces' of the Chinook. Its large, squarish shape tends to suggest to the untrained eye that this helicopter will be cumbersome and slow – misconceptions that the display pilot can put to good use! In truth, the Chinook is quite the opposite, being fast and highly manoeuvrable, the already good excess of engine power being made even greater by taking only a light fuel load of about 1,000kg for the display routine. The fast rate of roll is ably demonstrated by turning away from the crowd, into a 'wing-over' (from some angles it almost seems as if the aircraft has rolled completely) using 60 degrees' angle of bank and back to point at the crowd again – all in the twinkling of an eye. In the same vein is the Quick Stop – rush in at 140kt and 75ft, crank on 60 degrees of bank . . . a tight turn, the speed washes away, and by the time the 270-degree turn to face the crowd is complete the aircraft has come to a stable hover. As with all displays, there is no time to let the applause die away as the next routine must follow on smoothly . . .

The roll-on landing using only the back wheels, the reverse take-off and the Quick Stop are all manoeuvres which any squadron pilot could be expected to perform – most, in fact have operational usages. The main difference in the five-minute Chinook display is that they are strung together as a coordinated whole. Other elements, such as the horizontal spiral along the crowd line, have no direct operational equivalent – well, not one that the squadron has discovered yet, at any rate! By the time the display is over the Chinook is viewed with different eyes: it is no longer a sluggish crate with rotors, but rather a versatile and agile aircraft.

No consideration of the air display scene would be complete without a mention of the RAF's official display team, the Red Arrows. It seems that the average person at an air display would be happy to see only the Vulcan and the Red Arrows, and the long traffic queues at the close of a display are usually the result of the Arrows' being the last act and therefore of everyone staying on to watch them!

The Arrows are the latest in a long line of highly successful RAF display teams and in 1989 celebrated their 25th anniversary. Equipped with the superlative Hawk aircraft, the Arrows are generally acknowledged to be the finest display team in the world. Perhaps the most interesting, and pertinent, fact concerning the team is that all its members come from operational tours and return to operational tours; they simply stay with the team for up to three seasons, the length of a standard RAF posting. The basic concept behind this professional team is that it should act as a showpiece for the RAF by providing a display of flying skills which reflect the capabilities of the RAF's front line. Thus the team's nine Hawks perform a coordinated series of manoeuvres with precise close-formation flying and slick changes of position. The display slot lasts almost twenty minutes, and so each manoeuvre has to be timed to perfection in order to keep the aircraft in view for the crowd, with 'something going on' at all times – a hallmark of the Arrows. The other problem, of course, is that the British weather can never be relied upon to provide clear blue skies all summer! This is catered for by the team's having a flat, or 'rolling', display which can be performed under the cloud-base, and whilst visually this is not perhaps as spectacular it is equally demanding on the pilots. Knowing how rapidly the

▲ *The ungainly appearance of the Chinook is soon dispelled in a series of tight turns and steep manoeuvres. One of its specialities is the backwards-moving take-off, shown here.*

▼ *A formation take-off starts the spectacular display of the Red Arrows. Moments later, in immaculate formation, the nine Hawks re-appear over the crowd.*

▶ *The classic close formation – 'Nine Arrow'.*

weather can change, the Arrows can even transfer from one display to the other part way through!

One of the advantages of having nine aircraft is that more can be done with them: there are a greater number of formation options, and full advantage is taken of this each season. Whilst many of the manoeuvres remain the same year after year, there are always a few new ones to be seen, and the non-display period of the winter months is used to bring new pilots and new routines 'up to speed' so that from the very first public display the whole routine looks spectacular and polished.

To display any aircraft in a small area of sky for the benefit of someone watching from the ground is not an easy task. The performance seen is the result of many hours of hard work and practice, most done outside the normal operational spectrum as aircraft and crew are members of a squadron and have the same operational commitments and requirements as the rest of the unit. For a variety of reasons, air displays as we have become used to them over the past twenty years, are an endangered species. There is increasing pressure on resources within the RAF, and increasing pressure from without for reasons of noise and safety. Unfortunately, the many thousands of supporters of air shows do not appear to be as keen to press their views as their opponents are.

FINAL THOUGHTS

FROM THE MOMENT that the task details arrive at the squadron to the time that the last word is uttered in the post-sortie debrief, the crew of a Royal Air Force aircraft, be it the lone pilot of the recce Jaguar or the integrated crew of specialists in the Nimrod, has but one thought in mind – to ensure that the mission is a success. Every single flight is the culmination of all the many hours of training – the proof, or otherwise, that the crew, aircraft and systems can achieve the purpose for which they are brought together. The only essential difference between a training mission and a 'real' mission is that the former is flown in peacetime and the only threats it faces are the numerous natural ones.

Modern aircraft are complex items and are made even more so by the variety of equipment and weapons which they are able to carry. Nevertheless, the roles which they are called upon to perform have changed little since 1945. The chapters of this book have attempted to give a flavour of what it is like to fly missions – the thoughts of the Jaguar pilot as he flashes past his recce target at 450kt, the 'now he's there, now he's not' nature of high-speed air combat, and so on. It was never the author's intention to cover every single aspect of every type of mission – there are far too many variations and permutations. The essential point is that to have any chance of surviving and achieving the mission the crew must 'rehearse' in the most realistic environment possible. Flying modern military aircraft is far from being a 'nine-to-five' job: it is a profession which demands absolute dedication and the determination to be the best. The latter is given a boost by the ready adoption of squadron loyalty and the desire to see that your squadron out-flies, out-guns and out-bombs the other squadrons which perform the same role. You never stop learning, both on the ground and in the air: if you think that you can sit back because you know it all, then think again – you may be the best in the RAF, but are you the best in NATO? Training is a never-ending routine. Every mission in this book was a training mission, but could equally well have been a combat mission. We close as we opened, with the Top Gun motto – 'You fight like you train.'

▼ *Whilst the main body of the Red Arrows display team shows various close manoeuvres the 'synchro pair' split away and carry out a series of opposing manoeuvres before re-joining the rest of the formation for the finale.*